C000244644

THE TRANSFORMA
OF TA....

I had the pleasure in participating in one of Tiffany Crosara's Tarot courses to write up for Prediction magazine, her knowledge of and intuitive connection to the Tarot astounded me and completely dispelled any misunderstanding I had. If there is anyone qualified to write on this subject, it's Tiffany. Having spent most of her life working with this mystical system, Tiffany has a profound understanding of the cards, which she articulates expressively in a way that is very easy to grasp.

Gemma Birss, Deputy Editor of Prediction Magazine and Winner of The Frances Lincoln Diverse Voices Children's Book Award 2009

Tiffany explains her personal development journey with regards to the her Tarot abilities in great detail that many people could relate to and benefit from. As a natural intuitive, it is obvious that she feels the subtle energy of each Tarot card rather than just depending on the traditional meaning, therefore her translations are very significant to those who want to learn a new perspective of the Tarot. As a Tarot reader of 7 years myself, I would certainly say that her story and descriptions have already inspired me to delve deeper into the hidden mysterious messages of this ancient tool.

Sabi Hilmi, Author of *The Secrets of Angel Healing*— (published by Penguin in Feb 2011)

Tiffany Crosara is one of the best Tarot teachers and experts I have come across in years. She has the incredibly unique ability to impart her boundless knowledge of, and passion for, the cards to anyone who wishes to learn — from the complete novice right through to those who are already well-practiced and perhaps looking to gain clarity or brush up on their skills. We all know how easy it can be to get bogged down in this ancient practice, but Tiffany deftly unlocks the mysteries sleeping behind the Tarot's veil with a freshness and vigour that brings the esoteric art of reading right up to date. By giving each card its own fully accessible identity and personality, Tiffany will help you release your blocks and make friends with the Tarot for life.

Alexandra Wenman, Editor of Prediction

Tiffany is one of the most transparent and genuine beings I have come across. Her hard work, determination, integrity and authenticity are an inspiration. Books like these written by people like Tiffany are needed amongst all of the illusion and falseness surrounding this genre of reality. Tiffany is one person who does not make things up as she goes along; she embodies herself in her journey and shares her story with sincerity, telling it as it is. This courage and bravery to be transparent is what makes Tiffany's wealth of knowledge and experience accessible to everyone.

What I love about Tiffany's book is that it's not just about the Tarot, but it carries with it Tiffany's story and that is itself worth reading.

Simon Paul Sutton, Actor (lead role— Ao, The Last Neanderthal), Producer and Writer

The Transformational Truth of Tarot

The Fool's Journey

The Transformational Truth of Tarot

Truth of Tarot

The Fool's Journey

Tiffany Crosara

Hi Maria,

Welcome to The Transformational
Truth of Tarot! ☺
Enjoy the journey!
Much love
[signature]
x

DODONA
BOOKS

Winchester, UK
Washington, USA

First published by Dodona Books, 2012
Dodona Books is an imprint of John Hunt Publishing Ltd., Laurel House, Station Approach,
Alresford, Hants, SO24 9JH, UK
office1@jhpbooks.net
www.johnhuntpublishing.com

For distributor details and how to order please visit the 'Ordering' section on our website.

Text copyright: Tiffany Cosara 2011

ISBN: 978 1 78099 636 3

All rights reserved. Except for brief quotations in critical articles or reviews, no part of this
book may be reproduced in any manner without prior written permission from the publishers.

The rights of Tiffany Cosara as author have been asserted in accordance with the Copyright,
Designs and Patents Act 1988.

A CIP catalogue record for this book is available from the British Library.

Design: Stuart Davies

Illustrations from the Rider-Waite Tarot Deck® reproduced by permission of U.S. Games Systems,
Inc., Stamford, CT 06902 USA. Copyright ©1971 by U.S. Games Systems, Inc.
Further reproduction prohibited. The Rider-Waite Tarot Deck® is a registered trademark
of U.S. Games Systems, Inc.

Printed and bound by CPI Group (UK) Ltd, Croydon, CR0 4YY

We operate a distinctive and ethical publishing philosophy in all
areas of our business, from our global network of authors to
production and worldwide distribution.

CONTENTS

Acknowledgements

To my mum — Gillian Cobb, for being the one to bring life into me and Tarot into my life.

To my first mother — in — law Anne Ronald, for bringing the Tarot back into my life after the first rift.

To my father figure in spirit, John Waterman — for guiding me just as much now as you did then.

To my grandparents, for being amazing and so much more than meets the eye.

To my daughter in spirit — Lauren Ronald, for being such a powerful catalyst on to this path, and my biggest blessing always.

To my faithful friend Neil O Sullivan and his unswerving support and commitment to my path in its early years.

To my unconditional friend Steven Wilkes for being the living, breathing, shining example of a true spiritual teacher.

To Mysteries and the readers, for allowing me into the fold, for the magic which is Mysteries, for all the experience.

To Alexandra Wenman and Gemma Birss at Prediction magazine for their supportive comradeship and sisterhood along the path.

To Sue Bailey at Gateway for being the Gateway.

To Deborah Winterbourne at The Academy of Tarot— for sharing her tarot teaching path with me, and having faith in my unorthodox methods!

To Simon Sutton, Krishna Surroy, Isla Taylor, Natalie Virdee, and Kim Arnold for their kind, heartfelt offers and support on broadening my platforms.

To Patricia Finney, who generously gave her time to make sure this book got published.

To O-Books and my agent Maria Moloney Wilbrink for all the support in the process of publication.

To all my friends who have taken me in over the years, in

order to make sure I could continue on the path.

To my long suffering husband Richard Crosara— thank you. I love you. For your amazing patience, loving support and incredible acceptance — even when it must have felt like you were married to a hand! (The rest being at the computer or 350 miles or so away).

To my parents-in-law June and Laurie, for bringing such a beautiful soul into the world, and your support through our times of need.

To my beautiful step daughter Nicole, thank you for breaking my heart open, for bringing me into my essence, my truth, my love, my ultimate freedom and empowerment. May this book help you if you ever feel you need it through the twists and turns of life.

Thank you to all my clients — for all the magical transformations, for all the faith, fun, joy, respect and support you have offered so generously over the years, for being the reason why.

Thank you all, past, present and future, for walking the path — what a path it is!

Introduction

You have every reason to believe that your visions and dreams DO have the power to become a reality. What you are holding in your hands is the reality of my dearly held vision...

A vision I have about how one day the ancient and powerful Tarot may just be understood.

A vision I have about how the wise and enlightening Tarot may no longer be feared or judged. A vision about how the freeing and healing Tarot will no longer be shunned or misused, but valued as the enlightening and empowering tool I know it to be.

Far too long now, the ancient art of Tarot has been at the mercy of a crippling reputation. The fears grew from the seeds of strangling vines planted into our society and subconscious by the likes of Constantine fifteen hundred years ago. But now is the time to free our consciousness. The Tarot has been mercilessly misunderstood and misused. My aim is to release it from that stifling grip, and through doing so free a major aspect of our consciousness too.

The Tarot is an ancient part of our culture. The archetypes painted upon the cards are the gods, goddesses, planets and stars pictured for us to gaze upon as mirrors. In them, we can see our place in the Universe. They are little post-it reminders of our soul's path, an infinite reflection on the opportunities and possibilities within and surrounding us. Yet we test, fear and judge it. Judgement takes us out of the heart and into fear — the exact opposite of love. But Tarot is love from the Universe in pictures. We just need to understand it. When we have understanding, then confusion, pain and fear no longer exist. We wake up, see clearly, and only then do we discover our true free will. This is the gift the Tarot offers us, IF we understand how to connect with it.

This book was born to do exactly that. It will connect you with the Tarot through your own emotions, experiences and intuition. It will take you to the point where the Tarot becomes alive in your daily life. You will be able to see all people, places and situations in your life as archetypes, helping you to see the rhythms and truth of your life, as well as the rhythms and truth of the Tarot.

I hope you enjoy unravelling the mystery of the Tarot as you journey through these pages. But even more than that, my wish is that you finish this book with a new found inspirational peace and understanding in your life. For where the Tarot and your life are concerned (whether you know it yet or not) there is no separation.

With beautiful wishes for the rhythms/rotas/taros of your life—
Tiffany Crosara

Chapter 1

The Major Meeting — Personal Introduction

Looking through my very new four-year-old eyes I saw some really bizarre looking people lying on my mummy's living room floor. Well, they were little pictures on cards, they weren't really real — but they might as well have been.

I felt transported into their world as soon as my little eyes connected with their gigantic presence. The vibrant beauty of The Star in all her naked glory. The colourful freedom of The Fool. The powerful dynamo of The Magician. The deep otherworldly feel of The High Priestess was something I instinctively felt inside.

Have you ever looked at someone and thought "I know you"? Here I felt I had come face to face with my soul group. For the first time in my new four-year-old life I was not a little girl seeing with my little eyes. I had become aware of the old knowing of the soul that my young body housed.

It was the beginning of a beautiful relationship. Not an easy relationship, as a relationship of truth never is. But one that was to be the catalyst of so much growth it truly has been my longest, oldest, truest friend.

One that showed my shadow time and time again and tested my ability to face it.

One that whispered truths to my soul, and tested my ears to hear it.

One that trained my mental strength, as if I was competing for the world's strongest mind.

One that was there whenever I needed it, no matter how many times I disregarded it.

It showed me the forgotten power of the unconscious, and the forgotten weakness of the conscious.

It taught me the importance of respect and balance.

It taught me the painful difference between independence and co-dependence.

It brought deep vibrant magic into my shallow little meaningless life.

And it drove the truth into my bleeding heart like a stake, and tested my ability to feel it.

Like the truest of all friends, the Tarot taught me that if we look to external factors for answers we remain empty. But if we look at external factors as mirrors for ourselves we become empowered.

It wasn't until my teens that I embarked on the love affair. After the meeting on the living room floor, the Tarot lived in my mum's bedside drawer and never seemed to come out again. Of course, I could have gone in there and got them out, just like you would expect a curious little child to do. Particularly a curious little Leo child— curiosity killed the cat and all that. But I just didn't go there. I had no need or call to explore. I had what I needed, just through their presence.

Ten years later I saw them again, lying disregarded on my mother's bed like a forgotten lover. My mother always said they were for me and not her, but even before she voiced that I transferred them to my bed and the relationship began.

Looking back it would make sense that they had lain in waiting until the potent time of puberty. I now was searching, yearning, learning intensely. Trying to understand how the opposites of all life came together. It was so very dark and painful. I felt insecure, I felt alone. I felt totally and utterly worthless of love, my own or anyone else's.

Far from coming to my rescue, my new-found friends told me everything I didn't want to hear as I locked on to them and clung for dear life. They dashed my hopes time and time again, and I dashed them time and time again. Thinking if I consulted them again, they would tell me what I wanted to hear, I was astounded that time and time again the same cards came up. And scared too. I figured if that could happen, then what they were saying must be true.

That led me into an addictive frustrated fury of trying to cheat the Tarot into telling me what I wanted to hear. Oh, what an endless hopeless pursuit! I became sorely aware that if I managed it I was only lying to myself anyway. I became even more anxious, felt even less worth and felt even more alone. I couldn't understand why the friends I felt were the truest were torturing me like this. I became one of the hospitalised teenage Prozac nation. My stomach was pumped as a punishment for wanting the pain to stop, but being too scared to die.

I got out of hospital, threw away the Prozac and the Tarot along with it. But whilst something in my heart rejoiced at freedom from the Prozac nation, something in my heart sank to the bottom of the earth with the sadness I felt from being Tarot/friendless. It was as if I had murdered seventy-eight of my friends, yet I went bravely on, not admitting the grief I felt in my heart to anyone.

It wasn't until I was nineteen that my soon-to-be first mother-in-law gave me a deck of Tarot for Christmas. There was no denying how happy my heart was to meet her and be re-acquainted once more with my long lost "friends"?

Four months later I was two months pregnant and reading my cards. My "friends" showed me that I was to lose the baby. Once again, in anger and fear I disregarded them. Shut them away in the dark cupboard under the stairs, like a naughty child I could not bear to look at. I vowed never to speak to them again. I didn't tell a soul what I had seen, as if talking about it would make it real. Thirteen months later and the prediction was a reality. I was the living, breathing, walking, grieving archetype of Demeter in The Empress card I had seen, whilst my daughter was neither the living nor breathing archetype of Persephone (The High Priestess). Hades (Death) had taken her and this time there was no bargain for her to come back again. At least not in the world I was in.

Knowing I had nothing left to lose I began to tell people what I had seen in the Tarot. It was real all right. I could feel every ounce of that relentless reality pounding inside every inch of my beating heart, as it shattered every second with each beat of my being. Once again, trying to cheat the Tarot out of its truth had not worked.

You may have thought that that would be enough to put people off having their Tarot read for life, but quite the opposite happened. Intrigue spread and desire arose amongst people for me to read for them. I was hanging off the mountainside of resistance by my bare fingertips, while the people hung round my ankles. Over time, more and more people joined in, hanging round my ankles. I could no longer resist the pull. Once I sat there in the place of no resistance, the awakening happened.

If I could see all I had in the Tarot and live through it, then surely there was a reason for that? If all these people wanted me to read, then surely there was a reason for that? Was there a way I could use the Tarot to help people live through whatever they needed to live through?

I enrolled on a Diploma in Tarot. That Diploma was such a relief to me. I had found someone that could introduce my long lost friends to me, and tell me all about them. Oh my gosh, the penny dropped, and as the understanding grew it blew the pain right out of my system. The Tarot never wanted to hurt me. It never wanted my power. I just didn't understand it, like most of the world.

I opened my own centre in a deprived part of inner South London. The area had a strong Evangelical culture, and my practice was right next door to a methadone clinic and two minutes walk away from one of London's largest psychiatric hospitals. I had my work cut out as soon as I began to read professionally!

Some people wanted to persecute me. They labelled me a witch, a Devil, a portal for Satan. It became clear to me that I had to be strong enough to withstand people's accusations. I found a story from the Buddhist philosophy that became my practice:

One day a young disciple saw a group of youths taunt and spit at his teacher whilst the teacher was in meditation. The teacher did not flinch. The young disciple said, "They spat on you, why did you not retaliate?"

The teacher replies: "They did not spit on me, dear one, they spat on their notion of me".

My head told me of the bad reputation Tarot has amongst Evangelists. Experience taught me how strongly Tarot appeals to people in their darkest hour. My heart knew of the dangers it poses in that time. I knew I was in at the deep end, and I invented "The Three Golden rules":

Positivity Not Negativity
Healing Not Prediction
Empowerment Not Dependency

These Golden Rules came into their own the day a lady came in and said she wanted me to tell her where her head was. I asked her if she meant her mental head, emotional head or spiritual head? She replied, "I mean my physical head, they removed it in surgery and have hidden it from me ever since"!

Sometimes using the Tarot to heal rather than predict just isn't enough. Sometimes "healing not prediction" literally means having a healing skill you are qualified in so you can offer them that instead. Now I am here, writing this book for you. Even though my path clearly is one of liberating the Tarot and thus people through it, I have suppressed it for years. Even though my name means "Epiphany" and the truth has burned like fire running through my veins (perhaps left over from burning at the stake?). I am blessed to be able to dedicate my life to this path every day and I have simply practised the art of the teacher in the Buddhist story just told, without trying to convert anyone.

For the years that I have walked hand in hand with the Tarot (and as the years go on, the journey becomes more and more public), it is as if the walk is no longer the Tarot and I. Just the Tarot. People see me and they see the Tarot.

I feel I hardly exist anymore except as a mouthpiece for the Tarot. People want me to tell their fortunes... Fix their problems. Or they give me a choice of confessions — I must be a con artist or completely delusional?! I must "renounce my sin or burn in hell!"

Some friends saw me as a threat, one they had to beat down because it couldn't possibly be true. Others thought I was something special and put me on a pedestal, which I inevitably fell off.

Some stopped talking to me because they were scared I could "read their minds". Most stopped telling me things — they wanted me to tell them. Others saw me as a therapist or a party trick. Some family members just thought as I once did, that if they didn't mention it then it wasn't real.

Then there are some clients that come time and time again, in anxious obsessive despair. They are looking to the Tarot (as I once did) to tell them that everything is going to be okay. They are so caught up in the black and white thread of what is good and bad. They can't possibly stand back to see that these so called good and bad events are actually weaving the incredibly rich, beautiful tapestry of their life. So caught up in the thread, they wind themselves right up and even start to perpetuate their own mess. A thirty-minute reading every now and then doesn't even touch the sides. So why? Why do I do it?

Why do you breathe? Is it an integral part of your life? Does it make you feel good? Alive maybe? And when you do connect with someone to the point where your breath is one, does the euphoric freedom that comes from oneness and connection make living worthwhile?

These days I get much more pain relief from the burning in my veins by teaching people how to empower themselves. There is an old proverb that says, "If you give a starving man a fish you save his hunger for a few hours, if you teach the man to fish he will never go hungry again".

In empowering someone through to a new understanding, the gut-wrenching pain goes.

In September 2009, I told Spirit/God/the Universe that I wanted to write about the Tarot, my life and psychic phenomena (which is another book—and one this book touches on). I also said to Spirit/God/the Universe that I wanted to have the opportunity to teach more. I was exhausted from the intense pull of endless back-to-back, one-to-one sessions. By that time, I was a reader at the famous and very busy Mysteries at Covent Garden.

On one hand, I loved nothing more; on the other, I was disheartened. Some of the clients were showing addictive, obsessive behaviour and I was haunted by the feeling that I was just feeding it. I felt that I could do so much more, if only I could teach again.

One month later a lady landed in my life who wanted my services in her training school, which happened to be one of the busiest in the UK. Her school had never before ventured into Tarot and the psychic arts, which meant I had to write the manuals. That meant writing two manuals on Tarot and two on Psychic Development, and all within a season. This truly seemed to be my wish come true. The universe was making sure writing and teaching was coming into my life, inextricably linked. And so, *The Fool's Journey* documentation was born, which led to the birth of *The Transformational Truth of Tarot*.

Chapter 2

Tarot — The History, The Origin, The Word

Some say the Tarot originates from India. Others say Asia, Egypt or Greece. The truth is nobody knows for sure what are the Tarot's origins (I wonder if anyone has ever thought to ask the Tarot itself?). It is too ancient a system to pinpoint. Unlike Stonehenge or the Pyramids, it is much easier to transport and so it has travelled widely!

The Tarot has strong symbolic links to the gods and myths of ancient Egypt and Greece. Tarot decks through the ages have illustrated this clearly, "The Egyptian Tarot" deck, Aleister Crowley's famous "Thoth" deck (Thoth is the Egyptian God of writing, medicine and magic), and "The Mythic Tarot" deck which has an Ancient Greek flavour. Tarot has also been linked to Italy, France and the Romany Gypsies.

The recorded history of Tarot predominantly links it to Italy, where it was an early card game known as Tarrochi which the word Tarot is derived from. Tarrochi however, has no known origin. One theory suggests the word Tarot is the very clue to its origin. In Northern Italy a river runs, connecting Italy to Southern France. This is the "Taro" river. Does this map out the travelling path of the Tarot?

"Trumps" is the name given to each card of the Major Arcana. The word is thought to have derived from the Italian "triumph" parade. During this yearly parade, people dress up in costumes, bearing uncanny resemblance to the archetypes of the Major Arcana.

There are also Hebrew connections. The word "Tarot" is strikingly similar to the Hebrew word, "Torah". Translations for the word Torah and Tarot are the same: "universal law/book of life".

The Tarot has always been closely linked to the Jewish Kabbalah. The Major Arcana's twenty-two spiritual influences fit neatly into the twenty-two pathways on the Kabbalastic Tree of Life.

The Arabic word "Turuq" means "pathway."

First Exercise:

Lay the Major Arcana on the pathways of the Tree of Life. Where you feel they go (not where you think they go). Look it up afterwards and note the difference. What do you feel that says about where you are at right now? (You may not be able to make any sense of it right now, but as you work through the book you may have some revelations so keep a note.)

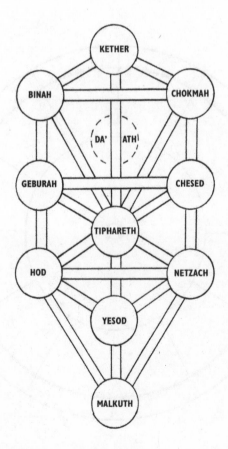

The Tarot's link to Astrology is shown in the anagram of "Taro" — "Rota" meaning "Wheel", an anagram of the prefix 'astro' where the letter "s" is missing. Astrology is as ancient as time itself, a practice that germinated when man looked up to the sky to make sense of the world below.

Astrology teaches us through the rhythms/seasons/wheel/rota of life, just as the Tarot does. Astrology has stood the test of time, just as the Tarot has.

Second Exercise:

Lay the Major Arcana out in a circle, in numerical order, and then look at the structure of an astrological birth chart. See the wheel?

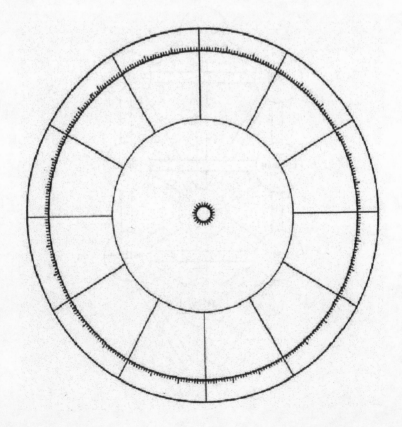

Another anagram of "Taro" is "Orat" — to speak, to tell, to share:

> The Tree of Life, Astrology, and the Tarot are not three mystical systems, but three aspects of one and the same system, and each is unintelligible without the others. ...the Tarot itself, with its comprehensive instructions, gives the key to the Tree as applied to human life.
> — Dion Fortune, (famous esoteric teacher and writer of early last century.)

Among the documented history, it states that playing cards first entered Europe (most likely from Egypt) in the late 14th century. Just like the playing cards today, they had four suits, Swords (Spades), Wands (Diamonds), Cups (Hearts), and Coins (Clubs). The very first documented evidence is a ban of this type of playing cards in 1367. Somewhere in between 1430 and 1450 the first known Major Arcana was added, also in Northern Italy. I question if this was the first Major Arcana as the Major Arcana has so many Egyptian and Greek influences. Another strand of documentation states that gypsies in 1781 were responsible for bringing the Tarot to Europe from India via the Middle East. My guess is that both versions of events are true, which suggests that the Tarot existed for just as long, if not longer in the South. It was French Protestant Clergyman Antoine De Court Gebelin who re/discovered Tarot's links to the ancient Egyptian pantheon of deities in 1773.

The Tarot survived through the centuries, although earlier decks were difficult to read. Pictures consisting of six wands, two cups or three coins and that was it! This archaic system was revolutionized in 1910 by Arthur Edward Waite and artist Pamela Coleman Smith who created the Rider-Waite Tarot deck and the pictorial key to the Tarot. For the first time the Tarot consisted of pictures that spoke a thousand words.

Waite was a member of the secret order The Golden Dawn, a

group dedicated to esoteric study. Not only did he revolutionize the Tarot with his fantastic esoteric symbolism, unlocking the sub-conscious of the reader, he also took it upon himself to swap two of the Major Arcana over. All decks pre Rider-Waite have Justice as the eighth trump and Strength as the eleventh. All decks post Rider-Waite have Strength as the eighth trump and Justice as the eleventh. Waite saw things in the Tarot, and his other studies that suggested the energies would be better expressed the other way round. The Rider-Waite deck has become the best-selling Tarot deck of all time.

The second best-selling Tarot deck, created in the early 20th century is Aleister Crowley's Thoth Deck. Crowley also commissioned an artist (Lady Freida Harris) to illustrate his deck, which is richly influenced by his travels and in particular his connection to Egypt. Both men's strong point was their esoteric knowledge and not their painting skills!

The rivalry that is felt between Rider-Waite's and Crowley's Tarot decks long after their passings, is symbolic of their relationship. Crowley was labelled the black sheep of the Golden Dawn and subsequently went on to form his own quite controversial orders.

There is no doubt that these two inspired international artists who have a passion for Tarot to paint their own Tarot or Oracle deck. I would go as far to say that everyday there are hundreds of Tarot and oracle decks being created. Even though there are many that are more eye candy than the Rider-Waite and the Thoth deck, these two really reign supreme as King and Prince of Tarot. So many have tried for the crown and subsequently failed.

Chapter 3

The True Tarot Deck

In order for a deck of cards to carry the name Tarot, it must consist of seventy-eight cards split into two decks: *The Major Arcana and the Minor Arcana.*

The Major Arcana

The "Major Arcana" which translates as "Major Box of Secrets" is a twenty-two card deck that pictures the twenty-two pathways (turuqs) that a soul must take throughout its incarnation/ lifetime. The Major Arcana illustrates the all important archetypes and "whys" of life.

It starts with "The Fool" — the new soul born into the school of life. The Fool meets a new self in each card/trump/archetype /pathway/turuq and progresses through each on to the next, even if it seems illogical. For instance the wise, old Hermit in the natural order of the Tarot comes six trumps before the not-so-wise unconsciousness of The Devil. Nevertheless, in the natural order of the Major Arcana, The Devil is still further on than The Hermit. It's just sometimes we need to go backwards to go forwards, so to speak. The Fool's journey goes on to The World (last card) and back round again. You saw this in the second exercise.

The Minor Arcana

"The Minor Arcana" which translates as "Minor Box of Secrets" is similar to the traditional playing cards we use today, as described in the chapter before. They represent the who, what, where and when of daily life. It is helpful to see the Major Arcana as "the puppeteers" who are playing the Minor Arcana — "the puppets". This means that you can read traditional playing cards as a Tarot deck, but your reading will miss the all important "strings attached" of the Major Arcana.

Any card deck without a Major Arcana is a set of playing cards or an oracle deck. Oracle decks don't require a prescribed nature, or two decks, and can lack the 'why' revelations of the Major Arcana.

The pictures in the Major Arcana may have contributed to the Tarot's fearsome reputation. Merciless images of The Tower and Death have people running in terror. The Devil card along with the Church gave the Tarot its nickname — The Devil's Picture Book. This happened at a time when the Church kept its power and order by driving the fear of God into the public. They did such a good job that the stigma is still deeply ingrained today. But as explained previously, there are also beautiful images of wonder in the Tarot. The Death trump does not actually mean death, it means endings and therefore beginnings too. The Tower does not only mean annihilation, it means the end of repression and therefore the strike of enlightenment and beginning of freedom. The Devil does not mean that you are evil, it just indicates that you that you are acting in an unconscious manner. The Devil is also called Lucifer meaning light-bearer. With the arrival of The Devil we are brought the opportunity to awaken.

The Tarot deck is neutral. Contrary to popular belief, there are no good or bad cards. Negative and positive lie within each and every one of the cards, just as they lie within each and every one of us. There is no point in wailing at The Tower as if it is some major destructive force, for it is also the beginning of creation (of what you subconsciously wanted). There is also no point in cooing at The Star (which comes directly after The Tower), because if you really want to catch The Star, you will need to let go of that to which you are still attached (stop wailing at The

Tower!). If you are going to use the Tarot in a deeply empowering manner, you have to understand this very fundamental
thing:

Everything in life benefits you somehow.

You have to understand this, for if you don't what hope have you
or your clients got? For the sake of yourselves and your clients,
remain neutral, just like the Tarot.

Chapter 4

The Tarot — Tool of Prediction or Empowerment?

Another thing that is important to keep in mind when consulting the Tarot is "The Tarot is a mirror".

The only reason the Tarot has the power to predict is because it mirrors back to us the predictable patterns we get stuck in. Therefore, you can use it two ways:

Prediction

The first way is to predict. Prediction is controversial. It can inspire fear and make people feel as if they have no power over their lives, as if they are doomed by some fatalistic power. In short, it can be downright disempowering. Some forms of prediction are illegal (such as predicting a death or an illness) and of course unethical. These days Tarot-reading is becoming a more regulated practice. Professional Tarot consultants are required to keep up with the forever tightening belt of restrictions and legalese. Be aware that although there are insurance companies that cover the Tarot practice, I have yet to find one that will insure the practice of prediction. While this is a step towards acknowledging the Tarot as a multifaceted tool whose talents do not lie in prediction alone, I am sure that the insurance companies are merely covering their own backs. The Tarot does of course at times reflect certain fatalistic events. At these times, it is important to remember two things:

1   Help the client to understand what is being shown, and why. For instance, just because someone only has milk, flour, eggs and sugar in their basket doesn't mean all they

can make is a Victoria sponge. They could make a pancake, Yorkshire pudding, batter or fairy cake. As an example, let's take a three card spread where someone has received:

The Ten of Pentacles, followed by the Five of Pentacles, ending with The Star:

We can see that their success has got as far as it can, (Ten of Pentacles and Five of Pentacles) and they need to embrace change (Five of Pentacles and The Star). Depending on how this is said, the client could see this as a fearful prediction of bankruptcy/ redundancy, or you can speak to them about how they feel in their career. It is more than likely that they feel the need to change, but the fear has kept the need only partially conscious. You can then counsel them in the ways of The Star — focussing on what opportunity the universe is now presenting them with. This way of reading comes so naturally to me now I hardly ever have to ask why the pattern has been shown, but if you need to, you can always ask the Tarot to show you why.

Secondly, just because it is seen in the Tarot it does not make it gospel. The Tarot is merely a mirror. The Tarot will mirror back a person's deepest feelings, fears and desires over and above their reality. Sometimes these fears and desires have the ability to inform and create our reality. However, sometimes they don't, particularly if the reality in question is reliant on another's fears and desires which are not in alignment with the original person's.

2   Therefore, if you see in the Tarot that someone's partner may be having an affair, it probably means there are trust issues in the relationship that have the potential to manifest as infidelity. Perhaps the person you are reading for has had unfaithful partners in the past, and now they have either locked into a pattern of attracting unfaithful

partners, or their fear of infidelity creates it. Bearing the brunt of the mistrust, the partner starts to "give up" and become what is projected or expected of them. This is a classic example of fear being given so much power that it creates reality. I was shown this very clearly when a couple going through rocky times came to see me separately for a reading:

One day a woman rang me asking if I could see a split in her relationship. Throughout the reading, I looked for it and could not see a split anywhere. In fact, the Tarot was showing something incredibly solid, the complete opposite of a split. The next day her partner came to me for a reading. When I dealt his cards, a split was written all over them so forcibly that nothing else could be seen. Basically, her desires were such that she did not want the split, whereas her partner wanted the opposite, just as strongly. The Tarot mirrored back their true desires. Alas, as they weren't aligned, their relationship broke down.

I continue to see this a lot with people that are fooling themselves with their relationships. The reading shows a rosy relationship that matches their desires yet next time you see them for a reading, their relationship has fallen apart (you do also get the genuinely rosy ones too, because their desire is aligned with their partner's).

There may be affairs you don't see due to the strength of a person's attachment and denial. Or the opposite may occur as touched on above — you may see an affair in a reading that could just be about an issue of trust. In the latter, it is the trust issue that would need to be examined rather than an outright prediction of infidelity. Even if someone's partner is having an affair, you will help them far more by changing their vibration of fear and distrust to one of love and trust, rather than prompting their fear to embed further and deeper with an ill-placed prediction. The

Tarot is not about being right. It is about helping someone understand their patterns, which leads us aptly onto the second way the mirror of the Tarot can be used:

Empowerment

Apart from prediction, the second way to use the Tarot is as a mirror. Like a mirror, Tarot can reflect back to the questioner the patterns they are stuck in. More important than the power to predict, is the Tarot's power to wake us up. Instead of looking upon what is shown as a fearsome prediction, we can look upon it as a mirror where the questioner can see and understand their patterns clearly. When we take out the fear, it becomes useful. We can raise our awareness and consciousness, which will lead to understanding and empowerment through free will. Remember I stated earlier that the Major Arcana represented a cycle of life, it just goes round and round, like our own predictive patterning. That is the only way The Tarot predicts, if we look at it as a mirror and change ourselves the reflection will change.

I also said that in order for a Tarot deck to be classed as Tarot, it has to have seventy-eight cards made up of twenty-two Major Arcana and fifty-six Minor Arcana. Well as far as I know there is one exception to the rule, which is the Osho Zen Tarot. The Osho Zen Tarot has seventy-nine cards, fifty-six of which are Minor Arcana and twenty-three are Major, which means there is an extra Major Arcana. This extra Major is called The Master. When The Master shows up in a reading, the consciousness has awakened to such a heightened level that we have freed ourselves from our current cycle, just as we will eventually escape completely from Samsara — the Buddhist word for the illusion and suffering of the world. This leads me on to one of the most commonly asked questions:

If I see something in the Tarot I can change it, right?

Yes, you can, but only if you see it clearly enough to know why it is there in the first place and truly understand that. If you don't understand why you are behaving the way you are then your consciousness is still relatively asleep, and whilst it is asleep it will continue in the same rhythm regardless of your efforts to change it. Free will only exists when we are awake. This is where the Tarot comes into its own. If you don't understand a particular pattern then ask the Tarot to tell you about it. If you don't know the best way forward ask the Tarot to show you. Most people forget to ask Tarot these very fundamental questions and ask fear-loaded questions instead. Asking fear-loaded questions for reassurance just breeds disempowerment and obsessive anxieties. This is not only the case if the Tarot is mirroring the fear, but also applies if it is mirroring the desire. Either way, it creates attachment, attachment creates imbalance, imbalance creates dis-harmony, dis-harmony creates dis-ease and dis-ease is disempowerment, a very slippery slope indeed.

I wish that when pregnant at nineteen and seeing that my daughter would die, I had thought to ask why, what was causing it, and the best way forward. But instead I felt doomed, paralysed by the fear of the prediction. Remember the Tarot doesn't want your power, it's you that ends up trying to give your power to the Tarot. The only way to avoid getting into a power struggle is to understand how the Tarot empowers you. With this in mind, let's now journey on to these powerful pathways of empowerment.

Chapter 5

The Major Arcana — Truth of Coming Up Trumps

The Fool's Journey — Birth to Adolescence

The Fool

O

The road that is built in hope is more pleasant to the traveler than the road built in despair, even though they both lead to the same destination.
— Marian Zimmer Bradley

Meet The Fool — His trump number is zero, representing the potential all and nothing. He is born pure, out of the cosmic egg pictured on the last card of the Major Arcana — The World. So here we are coming into another new cycle or birth/re-birth. The child of the universe. The child of the Tarot. The Fool is pure potential, freedom and light. Wonder and awe, all and nothing, all at the same time. He is the chaos theory, the big bang theory and all theories before. He represents birth, all things new, young and infantile.

Astrologically — The Fool is the air-governed sign Aquarius, representing how The Fool is as free as the wind and that he will go wherever it may take him. The planetary assignment is Uranus, showing the erratic, eccentric, unpredictable, impulsive, chaotic, original and innovative nature of The Fool.

Tree of Life — The Fool is found on the pathway between Kether (the eternal, spiritual perfection) and Chokmah (creation of energy).

Symbolism — is simple, just like The Fool! See below:

The Fool — the new soul on the new path, innocence, purity, naivety and ignorance. He is the child of the Tarot, so therefore represents children as well as general youth of life, births and starts.

The dog — represents the inherent animalistic base nature within, that is not so apparent as we grow. Note how it yaps at The Fool's ankles? Is his animal nature warning him or encouraging him? If it is warning him, is that a founded or unfounded fear? Who knows what lies over the precipice? If encouraging, is it because man's best friend knows that something beneficial lies just over the edge? Or is that wild, untamed nature destructive? This is a good example of the neutrality of the Tarot.

White rose — purity of heart, open and flourishing, tender and free.

Yellow background — colour of the solar plexus chakra, representing the will and the ego. Self-development, positivity, optimism, and learning.

The bag — he carries over his shoulder is black. Black in Tarot represents unconsciousness, so this symbolizes that what he possesses is unconscious. Where did he get these possessions if he has only just come into incarnation? Is this forgotten baggage from a previous existence? (Some children are known to remember their past lives and even hunt down their past life family members). Or do they just represent his experiences so far? They say that children tend to forgive, forget, and adapt easily. They live in the now, the most blissful nature of un/consciousness. It is also said that a child's experience can scar them for life...

The wand — the bag is suspended on a wand. The wand is depicted often throughout the Trumps. It is a potent symbol of power, conscious will and direction. Here, the wand is black which indicates unconsciousness. The way it is casually slung over the shoulder shows carelessness. Can you imagine the repercussions of not knowing you have a magic wand in your possession? One that is slung unconsciously and carelessly over your shoulder? Totally oblivious to the havoc and damage it may be causing as it is left to point and fire off in any direction, in reaction to any thought? Particularly if that bag is your karma hanging on the manifesting end! Well this is how most of us go through life. Like I said in the introduction, all the time the Tarot remains in the merciless grip of misunderstanding — so does our consciousness.

The cliff — represents anticipation of the unknown. To step over it or not? That is the question! Leap of faith or foolish move? That is the question! There is a thin line between bravery and stupidity. Does The Fool even know he is stepping over it? Or is it that he does not know the consequences of doing so? Is he completely and utterly oblivious? Is it a choice he is making? Does he feel guided to do it? Again, we see the neutrality of the Tarot.

Neutrality/positivity/negativity — All cards contain positive and negative elements, just like life. This means they are neutral in nature, as shown by the many double-meanings in The Fool. For example, just take another saying or two, such as "Ignorance is bliss" or "Ignorance is no excuse in the eyes of the law".

Bringing The Fool Alive

* Sleep with The Fool under your pillow and note your dreams.

* Carry The Fool with you throughout the day and ask yourself who and what represents The Fool in your life.

* What part of you is represented by the Fool?

* Do you love to fool around?

* Are you the eternal Peter Pan perhaps?

* How do you feel about responsibility, growing up or old?

* Do you always have exploration in your heart for new quests, places, people and projects?

* Do you have a thirst for learning?

* Do you love freedom and hate to be bound by predictable things like time?

* Is your home blown by the wind or changeable?

* Start something new.

* Go on a journey or an adventure.

* Connect with your inner child.

* Spend time with children.

* Allow yourself playtime.
* Practice being inquisitive.

* Practice following your hunches.

Notes:

The Magician

I

Character is doing the right thing when nobody's looking. There are too many people who think that the only thing that's right is to get by, and the only thing that's wrong is to get caught.
— J. C. Watts

The Magician's Trump — is ruled by the number one. The number one stands tall. Proud and independent just like The Magician himself and the wand he grasps. This represents the present moment. Consciousness and independence. Confidence, belief, will and ego. Initiation, power, and manifestation. Therefore also fertility and birth, literally and figuratively speaking — within the masculine sense of the word (Action).

Astrologically — The Magician does not have a zodiac sign assigned to it, however if I were to personally assign it a sign it would be Aries. Aries is the first sign of the zodiac, marking the beginning. Thus, it perfectly embodies The Magician's energy of initiating action. Traditionally, The Magician is ruled by the planet Mercury. Mercury rules communication and speed (our thoughts are fast in vibration). Therefore learning, travel, movement and keen perception, are the flavour of the day, along with eloquence and wit, and therefore trickery and cunning too. Mercury is known as the God of communication, as is The Magician (Mercury is the Latin name for the Greek God Hermes and the Egyptian God Thoth).

Tree of Life — The Magician is found on the path between Kether (Spiritual perfection, the eternal) and Binah (understanding, realization).

Symbolism — The Magician is packed with powerful symbolism that introduces you to all his secrets and his tools— The Minor Arcana:

The wand, the cup, the sword, the pentacle — All four "tools" of the Minor Arcana are laid out neatly and carefully on the table in front of him, ready for use/ ritual/ performance.

The sword — The element of air, representing thought.

The cup — The element of water, representing emotion (created from the thought/sword).

The wand — The element of fire, representing creation/action (created from the combination of thought/sword and emotion/cup).

The pentacle — The element of earth, representing manifestation (created from the combination of thought/sword, emotion/cup and action/wand).

Symbol of infinity — The symbol above The Magician's head is that of infinity, ever-flowing creation and energy. It represents the law of karma, cause and effect, connection and oneness; oneness, like his Trump number. Everything affects everything, we are one. The infinity symbol is placed above his head so we see that the power lies in our thoughts. Our thoughts (Swords) affect what we feel (Cups) and therefore what we create (Wands) and manifest (Pentacles).

The red and white cloak — Show purity and passion, the dual nature that lies in this card. Passion can kill purity, purity can kill passion. Both need to be balanced to work hand in hand, for good wholesome connected creation.

The wand — in stark contrast to the black (unconscious) wand slung over the shoulder in The Fool, here it is white, held with firm intention and consciousness. Here we see focus, will and intent. Here The Magician shows The Fool what he actually has in his possession and helps him to master his awareness. The wand is the will. The statement "as above so below" sums up The Magician perfectly, stating the power of the wand he holds is his ability to create. Because the wand is pointing upright, it signifies conscious intention and aligned focus. The Magician's other hand points toward the ground, confirming that what you think, shall manifest. The Wand is a symbol of The Magician being a clear channel to conduct energy through from the non-physical world into the physical world.

The snake belt — shows completion of magical energies, transformation, knowledge and will. It refers to the ancient symbol of wisdom — the serpent.

The rich nature — that surrounds him is a multi-purpose reminder:

1 Of the necessity of being grounded for manifestation to take place.
2 Of how health and abundance looks and manifests.
3 The red flowers show passion, power and action.
4 The white flowers show purity of heart and intent.

The yellow background — represents positive intellect, will, ego, sense of self and solar plexus chakra.

Neutrality/positivity/negativity — whether this power will be used for the highest good of all lies in how balanced The Magician is with his passion and purity. Will his ego go to his head? Does he become power hungry? Or will he use his energy to create consciously with far reaching vision, rather than seeing just "I" (one)?

Faith, integrity, knowledge and power, can all be used negatively. Blind faith, lack of integrity, knowledge for powers sake and power over others, can be used and abused for the disempowerment of another, which ultimately ends up as disempowerment of the self because we are all connected as the infinity symbol suggests. The dark-side of The Magician is consumed by ego, greed, vanity, and himself. He does not see (unconsciousness) or care (vanity/ego) that by acting in this manner he not only disempowers others but ultimately himself (oneness).

The conscious Magician knows and understands the laws of the universe (consciousness). He knows that what he thinks not only has the power to create, but affect others too. So he uses his thoughts to empower himself and therefore everyone else. We cannot empower ourselves and disempower others unless we are abusing power (which is not true empowerment but fear). By staying aligned (upright) to his truth, he empowers himself and sends ripples of creation throughout the universe, leading by example, working for the highest good of all and the collective consciousness. This is The Magician at his best.

Bringing The Magician Alive

* Sleep with The Magician! Record your dreams.

* Write verse about him.

* Carry The Magician with you throughout your day and ask yourself who and what in your life reminds you of The Magician archetype.

* How do you feel about independence?

* How do you feel about power— your own and others?

* How do you feel about the thought that the creation of your life rests solely with you?

* Does it scare or excite you? Do you feel empowered?

* Or do you resist it?

* Are there people in your life you admire or abhor who represent The Magician— who are they?

* Do you see them as vain, egotistical and selfish? Or as enlightened, confident and powerful?

* Do you or does anyone you know work in performance or communication?

* Do you or does anyone you know like to hold a captivated spellbound audience?

* Do you or does anyone you know live/work in skyscraper powerhouses, penthouses in city hubs or on leylines?

* Are you in a male dominated environment?

* Write down all you can about how The Magician manifests in your life.

* Learn magic/wicca/paganism or other earth-based practices, such as shamanism, dowsing and leylines.

* Develop performance arts.

* Attend courses or read books on intention, consciousness, manifestation and the law of attraction.

* Practice applying conscious action and focused will.

* Build an altar.

Notes:

The High Priestess

II II II II II II II II II II II II II

God grant me the serenity
to accept the things I cannot change;
courage to change the things I can;
and wisdom to know the difference.
— Reinhold Niebuhr

The High Priestess's Trump — is number two, moving on from the singular one we see duality in The High Priestess. The masculine phallic principle (1), meets the feminine gateway principle (11) the number two represents relationship, the nature of creation's duality, polarity and balance — the eternal yin-yang.

Astrologically — The High Priestess is the daughter of the Moon and assigned the zodiac sign of Cancer. The qualities of Cancer within The High Priestess are intuition, sensitivity, compassion and empathy. Psychic instinct, feminine wisdom, introversion, mystery and feeling. She is the ultimate in feminine energy. She is the triple Moon Goddess of the maiden, mother, crone. She is particularly assigned the maiden aspect.

The Tree of Life — The High Priestess is found on the midway pathway between Kether (the eternal/ spiritual) and Tiphareth (consciousness and harmony, the balance of the middle — beauty).

Symbolism — The High Priestess's symbolism has strong aspects to Kabbalah and The Tree of Life. She also represents the Egyptian Moon Goddess Isis (feminine aspect of magic), and Persephone in Greek mythology. In the Greek myth of Demeter and Persephone, Persephone was the daughter of Demeter (The Empress), who was kidnapped by Hades (Death), and taken to his underworld kingdom. Hades was bargained with, and Persephone was allowed above ground for half of the year when light is strongest — returning to the underworld for autumn and winter. She had already eaten food in the underworld — some pomegranate seeds — and so could not be completely released. The High Priestess represents the two energies of light and dark, consciousness and unconsciousness. The High Priestess is equally at home in both of those places.

Pillars — one black, one white. Representing the two contrasting, creative elements in the universe— the polar opposites. Upon the two pillars are the letters "B" for Boaz and "J" for Jachin from the Temple of Jerusalem. They symbolise the nature of severity and mercy (another form of polar opposites). The High Priestess in the middle of these pillars, show the need to listen quietly for our own sense of balance in order to create harmony.

The lunar headpiece — represents the three stages of the feminine, the triple goddess; maiden, mother and crone, the

growing, full and dying Moon and the feminine cycle. It represents her strong connection with the Moon, and all aspects of it.
Dreams, de-ja-vu, illusions, clairvoyance, lunacy. Repetitive
patterning and the past. Hormones, feelings, emotions. The
unseen and the unsaid. The secret. The eerie power of silence.

The crescent moon at her feet — (waxing/growing Moon)
indicates she resonates strongest with the maiden energy of the
young Moon, heralding the beginning of feminine creation. She is
the feeling state. The High Priestess shows The Fool the importance of remaining connected in balance to his emotions. The
Magician showed The Fool the need for thought in order for
creation to arise, but from thought arises the second vital ingre-
dient — feeling, which is our reaction to thought. Our inner
temple is a place we feel our way through. It is impossible to see
within darkened waters, or know their depth when the tide rises
and falls to the changeable rhythms of the Moon. This natural
rhythm symbolises intuition (literally — tuition from within).

Some of the imagery refers to the Catholic cult of the Virgin
Mary — which contained hints of many earlier Goddesses. Blue
and white are the colours of the Virgin, legends of her childhood
say that she was a maiden who served in the Temple in Jerusalem
and helped to weave the veil of the Holy of Holies, which was
mysteriously ripped in two when her son Jesus died at the cruci-
fixion. The Virgin Mary is often shown with the crescent Moon at
her feet, like Ishtar the Sumerian Goddess.

The veil — Behind The High Priestess (who sits guarding the
temple through her being and nothing more), there is just a very
thin veil separating the inners of the temple from your eyes. The
veil is transparent enough for you to vaguely sense the vast
embodiment of water behind it. Water stands for the sub-
conscious feeling states. The High Priestess is the guardian of this
subconscious pool; she knows it needs no action from her for

protection. Only those who are still enough, calm enough, and quiet enough, will notice that which is not immediately apparent. It is only those who can be, that can see. She possesses a deep understanding of the laws of nature and knows protection is a natural state when we are in balance. Therefore, The High Priestess is more a revealer of secrets to those that are ready, rather than a guardian from those that are not.

The scroll — humbly hinting in her lap, partly reveals the word Tora. As previously discussed, this important word means "book of the law'. Tora is an anagram of "Taro" — also meaning "the law of the universe/book of life, and "rota" representing the cyclic rhythm of life and nature. Finally, we have the anagram "orat" — to speak/tell/reveal. The scroll, being partially hidden under her watery cloak hints the way to find these answers is to go deep within. Listen to your in-tuition, these answers are not seen, but felt.

Cross — many theories abound the cross worn around The High Priestess's neck. Some say it's Christian, others Celtic, Babylonian, and some say it represents the Sun God. To me Christianity and Sun God for a Moon maiden really doesn't fit. The one that sits (like The High Priestess), or feels (like The High Priestess) for me, is the joining of masculine and feminine polarity in holy matrimony and balance, represented by the equal sides.

The cloak — decorated with many pomegranates represents the maiden aspect of the feminine. Pure seeds of potential fertility and creativity. Pomegranates are also a strong symbol of the myth of Demeter and Persephone. Within the inner pattern of the pomegranates, we see the shape and Kabbalastic design of the The Tree of Life, so intricately linked with the Tarot. Here the pomegranate is also a potent symbol of the seeds of life.

Black pillar — represents the underworld. The unconscious, unseen, shadow side, destruction and death side of life.

White pillar — represents overground, consciousness, illuminated, vision, fertility, creation and life.

Blue cloak — immerses her in intuition and feeling. Blue is the colour of the throat chakra. The throat chakra is the first spiritual chakra centre, after moving up through the emotional centres of the heart and solar plexus. This takes our minds back to the anagram "orat" and the spiritual communication present in the Tarot as a whole.

White cloak — immerses her in purity, virginity and maidenhood.

Neutrality/positivity/negativity — The power of our feelings can easily engulf us, just like water. We lose our footing easily, become consumed — particularly if the current is too strong or we are too rigid to roll with the tides. The High Priestess can be scary in her power and intensity, just like the sea. But without water we cannot learn how to swim, without tides we cannot learn how to navigate changes. Wherever polarity exists, balance exists. Wherever balance exists, imbalance exists. Just like the in and out flux of the tides connected to the ever changing Moon. The Moon is deeply connected to our ever-changing emotional tides. In order for mental and emotional balance to exist, does it have to be compromised? Within our dark inner waters we can become self obsessed, vain, depressed and paranoid. If we become unable to find the fine line between reality and imagination, mental illness can reign supreme through the sometimes turbulent journey of our emotions. However, through this we can learn to keep our head above water, to rise above the flood. Perhaps eventually, as the fear lessens we also learn how to dive.

One day, we may find we even enjoy it.

Once we learn how to roll with the waves, to be in the tide of love instead of fear, we can use the strength of feeling correctly, becoming truly empowered, healed and calm. In the flow of feeling, we are in touch with gentle nature, naturally intuitive, sensitive, compassionate and empathic to the point of being psychic.

Bringing The High Priestess Alive

* Sleep with the High Priestess under your pillow, record your dreams.

* Carry The High Priestess with you the next day to remind yourself of what people, situations and of your own reactions that fit her archetype.

* Meditate upon and write verse about her.

* What was it that made you pick up this book?

* What are your dreams like? Are they mostly day or night dreams? More feeling or visual?

* What instances of de-ja vu/strong unexplainable feelings have you had?

* How often do you feel pain— your own, others or the world's? Is it an emotional pain? Does it become physical? Where is it?

* Do you even know where your emotions begin and the others emotions end? Or are you a psychic sponge?

* What is it that maybe makes you wonder sometimes if you are going crazy, but that also knows something more that you just can't quite put your finger on exists?

* Is there a part of you that likes to retreat, be still, silent and alone sometimes?

* Do you have an ultra-sensitive friend whose moods ebb and flow with the moon or has prolonged periods of silence, either moodily or peacefully?

* Or perhaps that's you?

* Is your environment peaceful or watery?

* Do you love your home? Is it your sanctuary?

* Do you like soft flowing calming environments?

* How do you feel about water?

* Write down all you can about how The High Priestess manifests in your life.

* Take a vow of silence for a day, a week or month even! (Moon cycle)

* Practice developing your "Clairs" — clairvoyance (clear seeing), clairaudience (clear hearing) and clairsentience (clear feeling).

* Practice meditation.

* Practice being.

* Practice observing.

* Practice passivity.

* Make your bedroom into a Moon chamber.

* Plant a literal seed, or one of creativity.

* Practice being in touch with your feelings.

* Listen to your intuition.

* Enrol on a psychic development course.

Notes:

The Empress

333333333333333333333333

Without an understanding of myth or religion, without an understanding of the relationship between destruction and creation, death and rebirth, the individual suffers the mysteries of life as meaningless mayhem alone.
— Marion Woodman

The Empress's Trump — is three, from two comes three (birth). The one of The Magician has combined with the two of The High Priestess producing three. The result is creation, growth and abundance. The Empress represents the next stage of the feminine — the mother, just like the number 3 looks like a pregnant lady.

Astrologically — The Empress is assigned a planet rather than a sign, this planet is Venus. Venus rules both Taurus and Libra, hinting at the pleasing qualities found in this card. Taurus is a fixed Earth sign, representing the importance of a stable, healthy, solid foundation to build on— such as "mother earth". Taurus is a lover of sensuality, luxury, and aesthetics— as is Libra. But Libra is a cardinal air sign which brings in the all important flux and flow, so life can sprout through from a secure (but not stifling) earth base (Taurus). Libra also shows the important theme of others. Just like the mother, the theme of partnership, relations, balance, fairness, grace and harmony exist. In the Librian qualities of polarity, balance and harmony we see the qualities of The High Priestess, but now grown into The Empress. We have moved into the mother archetype from the maiden of The High Priestess. Venus itself shows the need for relationship, intimacy and emotional satisfaction. Desire is as strong as attraction. There is a need to be surrounded by all that is and feels beautiful and aesthetically pleasing if we are to feel comfortable with our surroundings and those that dwell within it.

The mother archetype is an archetype we rely on for life, before the days of formula would a baby exist without a mother's milk? No. Would we exist without the Earth? No. The mother has the power to create beautifully, or destroy. Sometimes destruction is necessary before new life/creation can exist, such as winter before spring (Persephone and Hades). Creation and destruction are two sides of the same energy. Just as destruction is a part of creation, Venus has a dark side that is mercilessly manipulative and destructive. This represents the dark side of the mother.

The Tree of Life — The Empress is found on the Tree of life between Binah (understanding) and Chokmah (wisdom).

Symbolism — Here we meet Demeter, the mother of Persephone. In The Empress, we are introduced to the first earth element in the Tarot. The symbolism is planetary, elemental, geometric and mythic as you will see below:

The green trees and ripe corn — represent the earthy theme, a healthy nurturing foundation and environment, which creates abundance, health, life and growth.

The flowing river — represents the feminine life force flow of nurture, of which she is a divine channel.

The shield — emphasizes the connection to Venus by being heart-shaped and inscribed with the glyph of Venus. The circle of the glyph represents spirit (the whole), which is being birthed into the physical body— symbolised by the cross of matter beneath.

The necklace — of nine pearls represents the nine traditional planets: the Sun, the Moon, Mercury, Venus, Mars, Neptune, Saturn, Uranus and Jupiter (Pluto was discovered at a later date and the Sun was regarded as a planet because it was believed to circle the Earth).

The crown — bears twelve stars, each one representing a sign of the zodiac. The soul births itself into and through each sign in order to grow/evolve and eventually stop birthing. The six points found on the stars are made from an upright merged triangle upon a downward pointing triangle. This is another way of representing spirit (upward triangle) coming into matter (downward triangle.)

The robe — Like the veil in The High Priestess, the robe is decorated with pomegranates, reminding us of the story of Demeter and Persephone, as well as The Tree of Life. The looseness of the robes suggest pregnancy: here we have moved from the maiden into the mother.

Neutrality/positivity/negativity — The mother archetype is the essence of life, is relied upon for it. It possesses an awesome

44

power. The power can give or take away. The mother can provide the very basis of love, security, nurture and support. Or she can cause suffering and destruction through withholding and withdrawing (or in the other extreme — smothering or manipulating). Here we see the neutrality of the feminine principle of creation and destruction. Here we see the Mother of The Fool.

Bringing The Empress Alive

* Sleep with The Empress under your pillow and record your dreams?

* Write verse and poem.

* Carry The Empress with you through daily life to remind you to ask yourself, who and what remind you of the archetype?

* How is your relationship to your environment? The earth? Your home? Your mother? Your child? Your inner child? Do they have flowing comfortable nurturing aspects or is there something edgy, rigid, uncomfortable or scary, about them?

* How do you look after yourself? Your nutrition? Your finances? Your health? Your emotional well-being? Do you nurture, suffocate, withdraw or indulge?

* How are your relationships in general? Would you say they are equal? Do you mother? Is there a manipulative thread existing on the fear of the creation/destruction principle? Perhaps they are closely-or inextricably linked?

* What parts of you are like The Empress? Are you creative? Do you like sensuality? Are you tactile?

* Do you have a friend that is pregnant? Creative or fits the "mother/earth" archetype?

* Write down all you can about how The High Priestess manifests in your life.

* Decorate your house.

* Get a makeover.

* Go shopping for decadence, art, fashion, jewellery.

* Do something for mother earth.

* Do something for the kids — yours or someone else's.

* Do something for your mum or a mother figure.

* Water the plants.

* Start an allotment.

* Move to the country!

* Open a savings account.

* Indulge!

* Hold a dinner party.

* Bring earthy overtones and natural fibres into your life.

* Go for walks in the park/country, take in the life around, sit with your back against a tree and feel its connection to the

earth and to you— turn round and hug it!

Notes:

The Emperor

IV

Either do or do not, there is no try
— George Lucas, *The Empire Strikes Back*

The Emperor's Trump is four — Four represents security. Four is a stable structure; tables, chairs and houses are all made from the structure of four. The Earth — a circle also needs four axis points to become whole. The Emperor is an inextricable part of creation.

In the Empress, we saw the flowing, natural growing energy of three. In the Emperor, we see solid status built from the man-made structure of four. The masculine principle of growth. The Emperor is the yang principal of The Empress's yin — the archetypal father. The Emperor stands for the external solid structure of the world — empire, authority, discipline, law and order.

Astrologically — The Emperor's planetary association is Mars, meaning the zodiac sign is Aries — the sign ruled by Mars. Aries is the very first sign of the zodiac, making it the very first of the fire signs. A cardinal fire sign, it shows initiation, full of power, force, energy, assertion and potent urgency. Courage, aggression, assertion, impulse, inspiration, passion, leadership, egotism, self-concern, narcissism, preservation and survival are all themes of The Emperor.

The Tree of Life — There are differing opinions as to where The Emperor fits on the Tree of Life. Before Crowley, The Emperor was assigned the pathway between Binah (understanding) and Tiperath (consciousness). But just like Waite saw reason to swap the trump numbers with Justice with Strength, Crowley swapped The Emperor with The Star on The Tree of Life. Assigning the Emperor the pathway between Netzach (creativity and anarchy) and Yesod (reflection and imagination). Please note that Crowley was famous for placing deliberate errors within his work.

His reason was to encourage the students to think for themselves. Is this one of those times?

Symbolism — The Emperor takes us to the next stage of creation. From the natural foundation, and nurturing supportive energy of mother earth, to the construction built upon it. It is said that Celts followed natural curves in the land for their roads, whereas the Romans were only interested in straight lines (the quickest most direct route), a stark example of the difference of expression within the same power of creation and destruction. In The Emperor, we see overtones of Zeus, the all powerful father God of thunder.

Barren domain — full of angular sharp and dry edges. Not a growth of tree to be seen. The river hardly flows. On one hand, man-made structures give us status, power and reliability, whilst squeezing the life out of mother nature with the other.

Mountain peaks — life at the top. Note that the higher the altitude the more difficult it is to breathe (starved of life force). It is lonely at the top, cut off and far removed from the rest of the planet/creation below.

Armour — stiffly encases a masculine figure. Symbolising the war father God Zeus, and the ever readiness to do whatever is required to preserve survival, even if this means doing battle.

The ankh — Egyptian symbol of life is gripped in one hand representing the power of life firmly in his grasp. (Note the similarity between the circle and cross of the Ankh and the glyph of Venus in The Empress).

The orb — resting so comfortably in the other hand, as if it was made to fit. The world, literally in his hands.

The rams heads — decorating The Emperor's throne indicates the qualities of Aries (as described above) marking his four cornered man-made territory.

Neutrality/negative/positive — Here we see the masculine power of creation and destruction in the father archetype. The Emperor is such a powerful initiator he has incredible power to sustain life through order. But the dark side embodies itself as radically tyrannical. So in control that power becomes out of control, unjust, destructive, selfish and restrictive. Here we see the father of The Fool.

Bringing The Emperor Alive

* Sleep with The Emperor, record your dreams.

* Write verse.

* Carry The Emperor with you throughout your daily life and ask yourself who and what is significant of that archetype?

* How is your relationship with your father?

* Who was the more dominant of your parents?

* How do you function under authority?

* How do you see the structure of society?

* Do you see any aspects of The Emperor in yourself? What are they?

* Are you currently building your own empire in your own way?

* Who or what in your life is representative of The Emperor?

* Perhaps you work in a city building full of powerful men? Perhaps you are one or an equally powerful woman?

* Perhaps there is a man in your life that is protective? Or a friend that is "typically male"?

* If you are male what is your relationship to yourself like?

* Wear red and note how it feels.

* Start initiating things, plans, strategies.

* Connect with your father/father figure.

* Take up a martial art or fencing.

* Tell your boss or someone in authority you admire their passion.

* Move to the city!

* Learn chess!

* Take the initiative!

Notes:

The High Priest

V

Nearly all men can stand adversity, but if you want to test a man's character give him power
— Abraham Lincoln

The High Priest's Trump — is number five (in some packs called The Hierophant or The Pope). Spiritually five is a powerful number linking the four elements of air, water, fire and earth with the fifth— spirit. In the Tarot, the number five is associated with a point of tension which naturally occurs when something merges and forms change. Five represents the halfway point within a cycle, coming after the even keel of four it shows the instability that is born from stability. Although fives generally represent a tough point of transition, they are to be welcomed, for without them there would be no progress. Fives are depicted by the Roman numeral V, the V shape can easily be thrown over, it rocks from side-to side in the flux of change. Unlike the solid four walls, four wheels etc.

Here we see the move from stability into the instability.

Having said that, The High Priest appears to be the most grounded and secure of all the fives. This may be due to its astrological association with the fixed sign of Taurus. In the V-shape of the Roman numeral we can see the narrow-mindedness and inflexibility of Taurus, we get the feeling that if we bent it, it would snap. Paradoxically maybe there is no sin more punishable than the resistance to change itself?

Astrologically — The High Priest is assigned the fixed earth sign Taurus. Taurus gives The High Priest a fixed, dogmatic, resistant to change (as described above). Endowed with a strong minded, stubborn and inflexible nature, we see the breeding ground of dogmatic attitudes. However, Taurus possesses an admirable determination, faith and commitment to patient slow growth. Also seen in Taurus/High Priest is a love of traditional values and protective qualities, deep loyalty, wisdom and knowledge. On one hand, the knowledge is shared generously for the good of community, but the other hand can indicate secret knowledge, or that things are held back for the self.

The Tree Of Life — The High Priest is assigned the pathway between Chokmah (creation) and Chesed (stability)

Symbolism — The High Priest relates to the male aspect of The High Priestess (also seen within The Magician). In The High Priest, we also see the spiritual aspect of The Emperor. Take the word "Pope" it means "father". See the Lord's Prayer "Our Father ..." referring to the patriarchal God of monotheism. (Look at The High Priest, The Magician, The High Priestess and The Emperor and compare notes).

The three tiered sceptre and crown — shows us the male aspect of The High Priestess. In The High Priestess, we saw a triple crown representing maiden, mother, crone. Here the triple crown and sceptre represent, the yang aspect of spirituality — father, son and the holy spirit. The sceptre indicates The High Priest as a divine channel, once again echoing The Magician with his Wand and The Emperor with The Ankh. The position of the free hand is reinforcing this principle.

Keys — hint that The High Priest has the keys to all the answers that people seek, the answer to prayers. It also refers to the medieval Tarot decks in which the High Priest was the Pope — and Popes have traditionally held the Keys of St Peter, allegedly given to the Apostle Simon Peter by Jesus in the Gospels, the power to bind both on earth and in heaven.

The lack of a veil behind — The High Priest shows him as ready to receive and reveal all spiritual guidance, wisdom, knowledge and protection (but look at how shrouded he is in what he wears.)

The pillars — In The High Priestess they are the contrasts of black and white, here they are merged, creating a neutralised grey safe middle road — and they look a lot like church pillars.

People kneeling — at his feet show the aspect of power and control. They look up to him as the safe pillar of society, as something special. They place their faith in him, that he has the answers and the power they can't attain for themselves. Here we see a power imbalance creating disempowerment and dependency.

Neutrality/ positivity/ negativity — Outside knowledge can provide education and security, but can be a grey experience. Cut off from our own truth and inner faith, it is difficult to discover the gift in ourselves. Our own purpose lies dormant and our own channel blocked. When one is brave enough dive into the depths of inner darkness (The High Priestess), the true power of light is felt (the dark and light pillars), catalysing the realisation of power within. We all have our own source, our own connection to "God." Our relationship with another is never the same as someone else's. If we give our power away, we become disempowered. The High Priest can stand for performance and cover ups, although contrastingly The High Priest also represents the grounded aspect of spirituality, keeping us safe and protected. The High Priest represents a time in The Fool's life where he has begun to emerge from behind his parents and learn about the structure of the world — the very beginning of change.

A great deal of the symbolism about The High Priest in the Rider-Waite pack refers to Catholicism — and not in a good way, but as a way of showing orthodox religion as an oppressive force. The High Priest is wearing the usual vestments of a Catholic priest and so do the two monks bowing before him. He is wearing the triple crown which was part of the medieval papal regalia and his right hand is raised in the gesture priests still use for blessings. The crossed keys are another symbol of the Papacy.

Bringing The High Priest Alive

* Sleep with The High Priest under your pillow and record your dreams and write verse.

* Does any part of you like to preach, pontificate, or educate?

* Do you or does anyone else in your life have a strong faith or belief that maybe unshakable or in danger of dogma?

* Note all the ways The High Priest makes his presence felt.

* Attend Church.

* Do something for the community.

* Hold a fund raising event.

* Study philosophy.

* Volunteer.

* Advise.

* Seek advice.

* Learn counselling.

* Teach.

Notes:

Chapter 6

The Fool's Journey — Adolescence to Middle Age

The Lovers

666666666666666666

Every decision made is a choice between a grievance and a miracle, relinquish the grievance, choose the miracle
— Deepak Chopra

The Lovers Trump — is the number six. In six, we have navigated the beginning cycle of change. We are moving on from the cloaked protection of The High Priest in trump five. We now take back personal responsibility through unveiling right down to the raw feeling of vulnerability. We need to truly feel the confusing depth of emotion when it comes to choice (the next stage of change). The Fool has reached the potent point of transition from childhood to adolescence. All sixes in the Tarot talk of experiencing final stages of change in order to grow.

Astrologically — The Lovers is the zodiac sign of Gemini, which gives us a clue to the real meaning behind this card. People automatically assume The Lovers is about love. The Lovers is about duality, and the heartfelt choice aspect of it. Here we see the quandary of emotion. The twin sign of Gemini captures this perfectly, representing the eternal quandary of being in two minds.

The Tree of Life — The Lovers are found on the pathway between Binah (realization and understanding) and Tiperath (beauty, harmony, balance)

The Symbolism — The Lovers echo the story of Adam and Eve with their dilemma about whether to bite the apple (symbol of love and temptation) or not. Choice (free will), was something given to us by God, but can be a heavy cross to bear. Do we yield to temptation? Make our choice with our heart or our head? Do we do our duty? Or fulfil our heart's desire? Unite the masculine and feminine? Or resist?

The angel hovering overhead hints at guidance, that the answer is to come out of lower self dilemmas and connect with the higher Self. Whatever empowers us also empowers others, creating a chain-reaction of highest good for all. The poised arrow shows the allotted time before choice is made for us; we may not like how it is made. Here the buck stops with us. The founding element in this card is dilemma, choice and the ability or inability to make it. The choice exists between the head and heart, duty and desire. Whether that be lovers, jobs, relations, locations, the list goes on. It is not a light or trivial matter but a true heartfelt quandary.

The change here has to do with free will, whether to bite the apple or not. We see The Devil here with the serpent round the tree. The Lovers holds a stark resemblance to The Devil trump, which is trump fifteen. In numerology fifteen deduces to six. In The Devil the choice aspect is hidden, but still present. In The Lovers the quandary is a conscious one.

Man — represents Adam and the active masculine energy of the universe.

Woman — represents Eve and the passive feminine energy of the universe.

Garden — Eden, foundation.

Crevice — Eruption of uncontrollable passion and destruction. Instability. Choice — which side to be on, do you stay where you are or make the leap?

Tree of Life — Spiritual learning through this necessary and unavoidable part of life. Pictured behind them it represents that they have all the support they need. It may not be obviously seen but the universe is supporting and guiding them towards making the right choices.

Tree of Knowledge — The experience will bestow on them great knowledge through this learning curve. It is a growing pain, a character building of which they emerge older and wiser. Once again being behind them, it indicates they have the knowledge they need. Again, it is not obviously seen to them, showing there is maybe a need to use hindsight or feeling to access the deeper, hidden parts.

Serpent round the tree — Serpents are powerful symbols of sexuality, temptation, esoteric knowledge and transformation. This symbol is multi-faceted, encompassing the points raised previously.

Angel — Divinely guided/fated element: Adam and Eve are so caught up in their **sixth** chakra , the third eye (balance and vision). And their **fourth** chakra, the heart (stability and love whichever way you count). They do not see the angel or the **fifth** spiritual element. They are only aware of an increasing feeling of change and chaos left over from the experience of the five. Nevertheless the angel is there hovering above seen or unseen, in the form of divine guidance waiting to step in. Some say the angel is Raphael linking the super conscious. Others say that it is Cupid, or Eros, symbolising that if we continue with indecision around our hearts desires then we must prepare to face the inevitability of the choice being made for us. That not making the decision is asking for the choice for it to be made for us (Cupid's arrow). Possibly that will leave us the classic issue of realising what we really wanted when it is too late.

Neutrality/positivity/ negativity — Destiny, fate, choice can seem like bad or good luck, but in life things that appear as bad luck often end up being a lucky escape. The only real negative side of The Lovers is not being able to have your cake and eat it — but we know cake isn't good for us, right? Addiction and drama are two themes in this card, themes that easily become out of control, exciting, then ruining. Remember, everything that happens to us benefits us, even if we can't see it at the time. As humans and Tarot readers, we need to look for what we can't see in more ways than one, in this way we build the knowledge. For a necessary initiation in life that we all go through for self-knowledge, there is no way better than to tug the old heart-strings. Here The Fool feels this in the potent onset of puberty.

Bringing The Lovers Alive

* Sleep with The Lovers (oo er missus) and record your dreams in a journal.

* Write a heartfelt poem or sonnet.

* Serenade and seduce.

* Take up belly dancing or snake charming! (Responsibility about getting bitten rests with you! This card is all about the buck stopping with you for your choices!)

* How many couples are in your life— what does their presence mean to you?

* Have you any heartfelt choices to make in your life, perhaps between your desire and duty?

* Take up Tantra or any other expressive partner practice such as partner yoga or dance.

* Pour out your feelings and dilemmas in a letter to yourself, in the reflection you may suddenly see the angel behind you and the way the arrow is pointing.

* Are you a conscious friend or lover? Are you aligned to the source of higher love or does your love come from the lower vibration of fear and manipulation?

* What can you do to help yourself feel clear, balanced and aligned? How can you help yourself stand in your power and take full responsibility for your decision/situation?

Notes:

The Chariot

VII

Freedom is born of self-discipline. No individual, no nation, can achieve or maintain liberty without self-control. The undisciplined man is a slave to his own weaknesses.
— Alan Valentine

The Chariot's Trump — is number seven. The Fool has acted on his passionate feelings of adolescence and set out on his first big venture. The number seven is a very magical number. Seven encompasses the four elements and the holy trinity. It connects the spiritual five with the soul contract of two, and represents the seven chakras and planes of existence. This shows The Fool that if he is aligned spiritually then he has all that he needs to succeed. However just like anything truly magical, the road is not straightforward. Many unexpected twists and turns lie ahead and success depends on the quality of his trust and faith. Sevens in the Tarot denote a time where trust and faith are crucial.

Astrologically — lots of people are surprised when I say that

The Chariot is ruled by the zodiac sign of Cancer, people often expect it to be Aries with its fast dynamic feel. Indeed, echoes of Aries do feel present and Cancer can feel too watery for a link to be immediately apparent. However, what isn't so obvious about Cancer is that it is one of the most ambitious signs, appearing to move sideways it actually knows exactly where it is going — straight ahead.

Take a look at the two sphinxes pictured on The Chariot, they look like they are going to the side but they actually pull the Chariot forward. It's still tough as the journey could pull you apart, but Cancer's tough outer shell shows the much needed armour and rock solid determination. Inside lies an inner softness and vulnerability amidst a turbulent sea of emotion. Once again, in the Tarot we are brought to the repetitive theme of reconciling polarities. Confidence without emotion is nothing but an empty shell, emotion without confidence is soul destroying. Confidence and emotion is the winning formula.

The Tree of life — The Chariot is found on the pathway between Binah (realisation) and Geburah (movement).

Symbolism — pertains to balance and unity of opposites. Uniting the two extremes to perfection for evolution (success) is a heavily repeated theme in the Tarot (especially in the Major Arcana). Is it that the Tarot is hinting to us the secrets of the universe? Like The High Priestess, do the secrets only reveal themselves when we have mastered the art of balance? Pantheon is represented by the young man in the Chariot. Pantheon was the son of the great Sun-God Apollo. He stole his father's Sun chariot in an attempt to prove his manly-hood. Underestimating the challenge of flying it successfully, he flew it too close to the Sun. The Chariot denotes a successful ending as long as we are aligned.

Crescent moon shoulder plates — stand for the tough, edgier quality of Cancer, as well as the much needed feeling state and guiding intuition.

Armour & shield — once again representing the tough outer shell of Cancer the crab.

Man/Pantheon — adolescent Fool stepping out into the big wide world for the first time, embarking on his first big mission — the journey of mastery.

Laurel Wreath — triumph

Wands — as stated in the astrological section above hints of Aries are found in this card. Here the wands are in reference to initiation as also seen in the first trump of The Magician. The very slight difference is that here, its primary use is as a symbol of will. In The Magician the wand is primarily a channel (although will is inextricably linked).

Canopy of stars — shows connection to the higher and The High Priestess. This re-iterates his knowledge of the importance of balance, showing that he has faith in himself and the unseen forces, or that the journey is about attainment of it.

Planetary headdress & clothes — nurturing support of Mother Earth/The Empress/The Mother, (third trump) reminding us just how young he is and where he has just come from. It is a hint of his inner emotion and vulnerability.

The city in the background — another reminder of where he has come from, now the sheltered protection of his father's palace.

The lunar faces — represent "Urin and Thummim" linked to the fifth trump (The High Priest). Urin and Thummim were the polar tablets of destiny (faultless or cursed) upon the breastplate of The High Priest of Jerusalem according to Hebrew Law (The Torah).

The two sphinxes — pictured in front of The Chariot — one white, one black, once again symbolising the opposing forces of the universe as well as the importance of unity. Is this the secret if we are to proceed safely & go the distance?

Yoni and Lingum plate on The Chariot — the Yoni stands for the feminine, the Lingum the masculine, represented by the red cross on the front plate of The Chariot. Coming together and unifying for solid progression, the nuts and bolts! (Look at the card). The combining of the Yoni and Lingum shows he has passed through The Lovers, maturing sexually he nears the end of the arduous process of bringing his passions under control.

* On the shield between — are the wings of:

* Caduceus — showing once again that by combining all opposites we transcend the power of life into pure creation, just as when the seven chakras are aligned we achieve kundalini awakening.

Neutrality/positivity/negativity — A challenging time for young Fool. This is his first time out of his comfort zone. He has been thrust into the exposure of the big wide world; no-one can do it for him. He has to do this one all by himself, with no experience to draw upon. If he fails to bring the opposing forces together, his ruin is inevitable. However, when we are responsible for ourselves then we know we have achieved. Here lies the golden opportunity of growth. In the Tarot there are definite fast and slow cards, this is not only fast but turbulent. However, unless factors aspect otherwise it is a triumphant card (as reminded by the Laurel wreath). The Fool is pulled through the challenging initiations of adolescence into a more confident adulthood.

The Chariot also refers to Plato's parable of the chariot as the human soul, struggling to control one white and one black horse, the conscious and the unconscious.

Bringing The Chariot Alive

* Sleep with The Chariot; record your dreams in your journal.

* Do you or someone you know put a brave face on things?

* Write verse or song about The Chariot and what it means to you.

* Do something to face your fears.

* Get out of your comfort zone.

* Go go karting.

* Ride a horse.

* Go to the races.

* Compete.

* Buy a car.

* Get clear about your path, aims, goals and where you are heading.

* Practice faith and belief in yourself.

* Make "where there's a will there's a way" your motto.

* Move!

Notes:

Strength

88888888888888888

Nothing is so strong as gentleness, nothing so gentle as real strength.
— St. Francis de Sales

Strength's trump — has been number eight ever since Rider-Waite assigned it so. Pre Rider-Waite, Strength was the eleventh trump. Number eleven looks upright, standing tall, confident and perfectly aligned, but it ends — **11. 8** never ends, just like the symbol of infinity, a symbol of a connection to the source, never depleting or ending. Eight possesses such a gentle flowing strength of connection that it does not need to make a tall statement like eleven. True strength comes from being comfortable in oneself, no matter how the outside manipulates or pounds you, you simply adjust and bounce back. Nothing can disconnect you; flow is constant. Each of us is connected to that source, deep down within a part of each and everyone remains untouched and is always okay. This soft, flowing analogy demonstrates that real strength cannot be toppled or broken.

Eleven (just like pillars) can.

Astrologically — Strength is assigned the ruler of the zodiac, Leo. Leo is ruled by our ruling planet the Sun. As the Sun is the centre of our solar system it is sometimes known as the source, everything magnetically revolves around it. The Sun is pure source, and that is attractive, it is untouchable in its extreme source of light and power.

Clouds move in front of the Sun, but the Sun doesn't fight the clouds as it knows nothing can threaten its existence, it remains untouched. The Sun knows that its essence will continue to shine on infinitely, no matter what. In The Chariot, we find a forced strength which is called control. In Strength The Fool finds himself a world away from the adrenalin fuelled challenge of The Chariot, even though we are just one step away. In The Chariot, there is challenge, something to prove, to fight for. In Strength The Fool has arrived at a place of deep inner knowing. The Chariot, albeit opposite to Strength is not weak. The Chariot ruled by Cancer, ruled by the Moon, is the other most dominating planet in our sky, the opposite of our Sun (but illuminated by it). Cancer stands for the tough outer shell. Leo stands for the ability to shine infinitely from the source with a gentle warmth, grace and ease.

Tree of Life — Strength is found on the pathway between Geburah (movement and power) and Tiperath (consciousness).

Symbolism — Strength is the first of the four virtues. The Four Virtues can be seen as cornerstones of the Tarot. Strength, as we discussed above relates to the Sun. The Sun is a big yellow spinning disc, just like the solar plexus chakra. The overall yellow depicted in the Strength card tells of a totally radiant and healthy solar plexus, the centre is the key to the source. Psychic cords can be found in this very chakra if anyone tries to manipulate you, but when it is strong, healthy and radiant it remains untouchable like the Sun.

The lady — is in the courageous act of opening a Lion's jaw. Obviously, it's a feat that wouldn't be attempted without complete courage of conviction. This is something so brave it may be stupid. But the lady is not risking a thing because she has absolutely no doubt she can succeed. She does not think she can succeed. She knows. Consequently, the Lion feels the power of her will and submits accordingly. There is no need to force the Lion's mouth open, there is nothing to prove. She only has purity in her heart as pictured by the white robe. Her serene face, childlike in naivety is accomplishing a triumph that adults would quake to face. Her innocence does not realise what a feat it is. This is the true power of the universe, with calm focus, centred presence and inner knowing, anything be accomplished through the strength of gentleness.

Symbol of infinity — present also in The Magician. It is the power within that creates manifestation. In Strength, we see those echoes in the softer feminine form. It shows the magic ability of connection and the unbreakable endurance of eight.

Neutrality/negativity/positivity — Strength is known to be one of the most positive trumps indicating you have all you need to succeed. Nevertheless, remember all cards are neutral. The Strength card may assure like no other that you possess all you need to shine and succeed, but how would The Fool know the depth of his strength if he hadn't come face to face with the Lion?

Bringing Strength Alive

* Place the Strength card under your pillow and note your dreams.

* Write verse on the Strength card.

* List your strengths.

* List your weaknesses — then look at how they are Lions helping you to grow strong.

* List people you admire for the graceful way they conduct themselves in adversity, whether it be Gandhi or your next-door neighbour.

* List the people who challenge you — and why? How are they your Lions?

* Practice shining your light to illuminate the world rather than hiding it under a bushel.

* Practice feeling that subtle gentle strength that emerges through vulnerability.

* Allow your inner child out to play, fearlessly for living in the moment.

* Watch inspirational films and read inspirational books.

* Practice gentle connective meditation.

Notes:

The Hermit

THE HERMIT.

999999999999999

Have patience with all things, but chiefly have patience with yourself. Do not lose courage in considering your own imperfections but instantly set about remedying them — every day begin the task anew.

— Saint Francis de Sales

The Hermit's Trump — is number nine. In nine, The Fool is approaching the end of his first cycle, which ends with ten. Any nine in the Tarot represents the nearing of the end of a cycle. That cycle can either be light or heavy in nature, depending on the suit or element. In The Hermit, we see The Fool going through his rite of passage into adulthood. If we look at The Hermit, he stands 9-shaped, tall with hooded head and lit lantern, turning back in on himself.

Astrologically — The Hermit represents the analytical earthy quality of Virgo. Virgo is an earth sign but ruled by Mercury; through Mercury, we see the element of air/thought showing us the mind aspect of Virgo. Virgo is known as one of the most analytical zodiac signs. Thought is one of the finest, fastest frequencies there is, but The Hermit is one of the slowest cards in the Tarot! To me The Hermit feels Saturnian in nature, (slow and earthy) in which case we are seeing the combination of earth and air. Earth is the slowest, densest, frequency in our universe, so here we see a slowing down of thought into the deep, dense, analytical state. It is no coincidence that The Hermit is linked to the Saturn return. The Saturn return is an astrological transit, which happens every twenty-eight years and lasts for two. Saturn (known as the hard taskmaster) makes us take a good long hard look at ourselves, ripping off the rose-tinted glasses. Saturn makes us see reality for what it is, so we can truthfully assess our path ahead. Saturn is also known as the lord of karma, karmic relationships and past-life situations can be triggered here. We are pulling back to build momentum for forward swing. Saturn has a third name too — the lord of dreams. This tells us that if we work diligently with patience through this long, slow arduous and sometimes dark energy, our experience becomes the very material of our dreams. It is the true alchemical process. Saturn return is a test of your ore in the fires, a rite of passage, a sharp learning curve and a character building assessment. At this point The Fool grows up and realises how little he knew. Any trace of naivety left in Strength is gone and a weathered, beaten maturity enters. Now we enter a deep karmic phase that lasts for some time, as you will see in the following trumps.

Tree of Life — The Hermit is found on the path between Chesed (growth and stability) and Tiperath (consciousness and harmony).

Symbolism — The Hermit is the second of the four virtues, Patience, the second cornerstone. Here we see the monk and alchemist. The earthiness and greyness symbolise the slow movement of the old grey matter!

The mountain — The Hermit stands at the peak of the mountain, showing how far he has come. Now he has reached a still point he must take time to reflect on his journey and integrate what he has learnt if he is to move on successfully.

The staff — represents sturdy, reliable support (if dug in slowly and surely).

Illustration 66 here*The lantern* — shows he possesses the illumination necessary. In the Rider-Waite deck, it is shown as a star captured by the bars of the lantern for the Hermit to study. The pose echoes some of the paintings of Father Time, holding an hourglass rather than a lantern.

The grey background — represents a time not for exposure in the buoyant yellow of Strength, but quiet, reflective hibernation.

Neutrality/negativity/positivity — The Hermit is so very slow that he has not just stopped, he is going back, back over all his life experience so far. Not from nostalgia, but with a driven determination to understand, integrate and transform. One of the slowest cards in the Tarot, often met by groans and protests by clients of "I have no patience"! The Hermit will make sure you do!

Bringing The Hermit Alive

* Sleep with The Hermit under your pillow and note your experience.

* Write verse on The Hermit.

* Do you or someone you know constantly fall into a cycle of serious over analysation of everything?

* Are you introverted or extroverted?

* Do you groan at challenges or welcome the experience?

* Is there a wise old man archetype in your life?

* Write down all the ways you can see The Hermit in your life

* Go mountaineering — slowly.

* Turn your phone off and spend the day in bed reflecting.

* Retreat — or go on one.

* Go for a Past Life Regression.

* Reflect over past cycles and see if you can gain clarity on the reason for them, and what they have taught you.

* Take a vow of silence.

* Meditate.

* Undertake Vipassana.

* Visit a monastery.

* Visit a cave.

* Take a course in philosophy.

* Research.

Notes:

The Wheel of Fortune

10101010101010

How people treat you is their karma; how you react is yours
— Wayne Dyer

The Wheel's Trump — is number ten. In ten, we reach the end of a cycle. The end of one is always the start of another, **1** — commencement, **0** — cycle. This sounds like a starting point but really we are looking at the ending point prior to the start, even so you can't have an end without a start!

The Fool has completed his first trip round The Wheel marking the great change emerging from the inner quest of The Hermit.

Astrologically — The Wheel represents the zodiac itself, a gigantic wheel upon which the time and place we are born becomes etched in our destiny/karma/fate. The Wheel, whether it be the zodiac or The Wheel of Fortune, shows us where we are in our cycles of evolution. Aries is the first sign of the zodiac representing the new soul. Aries learns from Taurus, Taurus learns from Gemini and so we go round the wheel until quite a few lives later we reach Pisces. Pisces is the old soul, the final step in evolution. In Pisces, we see the escape of Samsara which is the ongoing wheel of life known in Buddhist traditions. (Please note this doesn't mean that all Aries are immature and every Piscean wise!) In order to know accurately where we are on The Wheel the whole birth chart (The Wheel) has to be studied. The whole wheel equates the whole picture.

The Wheel is associated with Jupiter, known as an expansive, lucky planet. Jupiter is called the major benefic in Astrology, stark in contrast to the trump before being ruled by Saturn, a planet known as the major malefic. So where does the luck element come from? The Wheel is karmic.

What may appear as luck, be it good or bad, may actually be karma from previous turns/lives on The Wheel.

Being karmic The Wheel marks a significant and important turn of events, these events are known as transits within astrology. The Saturn Return is one of the most significant, occurring from the age of twenty-eight until thirty and fifty-six until fifty-eight. One of the other most major (if not the major) is the Uranus Opposition. Labelled the mid-life crisis in society, the Uranus Opposition is the astrological reason behind it. This transit starts at thirty-eight and ends at around forty. The next significant one is the Chiron Return starting at fifty. Then the Uranus Return from seventy-eight, which may well be our last, just like the seventy-eight cards in the Tarot. The changes that arise from these transits aren't something fresh but born out of past actions/karma.

The Wheel is also assigned the four fixed signs of the zodiac as four points make a wheel (we also see this in the roman numeral for ten — x) The points/signs are Aquarius, Taurus, Leo and Scorpio. In The Wheel card, the angel represents Aquarius. Taurus is of course the bull. Leo the lion and Scorpio is the eagle, which was the representation for Scorpio before the scorpion. All four ancient astrological archetypes are seen with wings; introducing the biblical story of Ezekial. Ezekial has a vision of God in a spectacular chariot drawn by a lion, eagle, man and bull. In this vision, God commissions Ezekiel to be a watchman and prophet for Israel. In Christian symbolism, these beings mean the Gospel-writers — Matthew, Mark, Luke and John — which is why they are all shown with the wings of spirit and all hold a book.

The four signs mark the four turning points; four quarters are present in all wheels. Take a look at the wheel of the year, it is divided into four quarters known as seasons, each season has a turning point (equinox or solstice). Each of the four astrological signs represent one of the four elements: Taurus (Earth), Leo (Fire), Scorpio (Water) and Aquarius (Air). These elements make a whole/a circle/a wheel/a completion/a cycle.

The symbols written upon the spokes are alchemical, linked to the elements (as The Hermit can be linked to the Alchemist). Starting from the top and going clockwise they read as mercury, sulphur, water and salt; combining these four elements produces the spiritual fifth.

The Tree of Life — The Wheel is found on the pathway between Chesed (power of growth) and Netzach (creativity and anarchy)

Symbolism — as you have probably gathered The Wheel bursts with symbolism. The symbolism is biblical, kabbalistic, astrological and Egyptian in nature. All of which are all powerful, ancient and incredible systems of spiritual revelations.

The Wheel — the letters T A R O (laws of the universe) are embossed upon it, we have seen this word before in The High Priestess. The letters T A R O can also be read as R O T A meaning wheel. And TORA which stands for Torah showing the Hebrew connections through the Kabbalah. The letters in-between are Y H V H; these represent the true name of God within the

Kabbalah. Without vowels it is unpronounceable, symbolising that man's limited use of words are unworthy of the true name of God. Our understanding and vocabulary fall short. Reminding us the law of the universe is way too expansive to be containable within a human mind/structure.

The snake — descending the wheel is Seth, the Egyptian God of death.

The Jackal headed figure — transcending The Wheel is the Egyptian God Anubis. Anubis is a guide to the dead, just like the ten, he is also the bringer of new life.

The Sphinx — on the top of The Wheel represents perfect resurrection. Ongoing life through creation, destruction and re-creation, which pictures perfectly the karmic nature of The Wheel.

Neutrality/positivity/negativity — the main influence of The Wheel is beneficial due to its assignment with Jupiter. Great opportunity can be present within this card but it also tells of the reaping of what The Fool has sown, whether reaping reward or paying back; facing up to past actions, whether they were good or bad. To me the expansiveness of Jupiter is more constant than the luck element. They say karma has a habit of coming back three fold; this represents the expansiveness of Jupiter perfectly, presenting opportunity for growth, either through gifted opportunities or learning from past actions. The Wheel is cyclical in nature and has a high point and a low point. In life, the only constant is that everything changes. Through that, hopefully we get to see the whole/bigger picture.

Bringing The Wheel Alive

* Sleep with The Wheel under your pillow and note your dreams.

* Write verse.

* Paint your own mural/wheel/mandala.

* What's your favourite and least favourite time of the year and why?

* How do you see the nature of life? Is it all down to luck? Do you feel born lucky or unlucky? Is it Karmic or fated? Destined? Or are we responsible for our own luck?

* How do you see life? Is it a mixture of good and bad experiences? Or do you see that all experiences are about learning something for progression and advancement?

* What's your star sign? Are you one of the four fixed signs? Do you feel fixed/strong minded/ stuck/habitual/stubborn maybe?

* How do you relate to the other four fixed signs? Who are they in your life?

* How many cycles do you feel you have had in your life so far? How old were you at each?

* Write down all the ways you can see The Wheel in action in your life.

* Get your birth chart done and study it.

*   Read the biblical story of Ezekial.

*   Learn astrology.

*   Study the seasons.

*   Think about how everything you do is connected, every action has a reaction. Where did you buy your eggs? Your chocolate? Your coffee? Your clothes? Where did they come from? Somewhere/someone empowered, or disempowered? What turn of The Wheel are you supporting for others?

Notes:

Justice

111111111111111

*There is a higher court than courts of justice and that is the court of
conscience. It supersedes all other courts.*
— Gandhi

Justice is trump — number eleven. Pre Rider-Waite it was trump
eight (as discussed in Strength). Eight represents karmic retri-
bution of cause and effect; eleven represents upright pillars of
Justice. So here it seems we have dilemma — a common theme of
Justice! However eleven wins when we look at the energy of
graceful Strength and the numerology of eleven. Eleven reduces
to two, take that down further we end with one, this shows us the
presence of the all-knowing High Priestess, combined with the
confident assertion of The Magician, a powerful combination.
Look underneath the title of Justice and you will see the way I
chose to symbolise Justice. I used the same representation before
in The High Priestess and The Magician.

Astrologically — Justice is Libra balancing the scales of moral diplomacy. Having the vision to see what isn't obvious (The High Priestess), the Strength (Trump 8) to face the truth and the confidence to act on the findings (The Magician). Libra is the sign of service, always striving for perfect balance, resolution and harmony. Half way round the zodiac wheel (The Wheel Of Fortune) from the first sign of Aries (self) here we see the half way point of the journey as an opposite (service).

Tree of Life — Justice is found on the pathway between Geburah (power of destruction and movement) and Chesed (power of growth and stability).

Symbolism — In Justice we meet the third virtue. The quality of strength and virtue of patience are being combined to produce Justice. The prior passage of The Wheel ignited consciousness of cause and effect, arriving now at karmic accountability.

In Egyptian Mythology, Justice is the Egyptian Goddess Matt. Matt weighed human hearts against a feather to determine whether the soul was light enough to enter the next realm. In Greek mythology, Justice is the warrior Goddess Athena who fights for what is right. The colour purple found in Justice (it looks like red in the Rider-Waite) signifies the coming together of the masculine/active principle (red) and feminine/passive principle (blue). Active and passive in perfect balance create deep wisdom (violet).

The figure — is seated in between the two pillars (11) of severity and mercy, just like The High Priestess. Except here, the pillars are both grey instead of one black and one white, picturing merging of the opposites into balance within the material realm.

Scales — perfectly balanced, fairness and unity.

The upright sword — The power of clear thought, straight up vision, sharp judgements, clear communication and cutting accountability. Balanced rationality and sharp insight slice right through illusion. The Sword of Justice implies the power to execute the guilty and was always held upright.

The purple veil — Just like in The High Priestess we see a veil, but here the veil is not see-through. It is a deep solid purple. As discussed previously purple is the combination of blue (passivity) and red (action). The perfect clear balance of both these aspects merge into wisdom, this wisdom is solid (solidarity).

The red robe — A cloak of courageous strength determined to apply the correct course of action.

The yellow crown — shows a clear, strong, and knowledgeable intellect.

Neutrality/positivity/negativity — This card cannot be tempted into manipulative bribery, it holds no special favours for status. We are all the same in the eyes of a correct just law. Ignorance is no excuse as we know in our worldly law, but this theme carries further into spiritual law.

Justice will always be done, if not this lifetime, then next. The karmic theme continues, which can be seen in human eyes as positive or negative. However, you choose to see it, there is no getting away from fact. Justice is a mentor, a guide, a teacher.

Her judgements become a measure for our success, a structure to gain the necessary wisdom. She enables us to take responsibility (ability to respond), act in accountability (ability to account) and be in line with our highest self (integrity). Our coming into balance results in freedom from the prison sentence of the past.

In order to do this, we need to be truly honest with ourselves, which may never be as easy as it sounds. In order to do that we have to face deep truths we may rather not face. But if we deceive ourselves, we deceive others, creating a domino effect of dishonesty, disharmony and disempowerment.

Without Justice, we create a trail of karmic destruction. Domino karma gets stronger and stronger the longer the knock on effect is left. Harsh truths will need to be faced for an ultimate clearing of karma. In The High Priestess, things were subtle and not completely revealed. Here they are, loud and clear.

Bringing Justice Alive

* Sleep with Justice and note your dreams.

* Write verse.

* How well do you know yourself?

* Do some questionnaires/personality quizzes.

* Can you face the truth about yourself?

* Make a list of all the things you love and things you would like to improve about yourself for yourself and for your relationships, and be honest!

* Do you know someone with strong morals, integrity or judgements?

* Is there someone around you who is involved in the law or another pillar of society?

* How do you feel about the Law?

*   Or the universe? What are your personal dealings with it? Do you feel supported or injusticed? If injusticed maybe it's time for a past life regression to see why?

*   Study Law or Politics.

*   Become a pillar of society.

*   Study your relationships, they are a mirror, what do they tell you?

*   Are you living your life honestly?

*   Are you earning your living honestly?

*   Write down all the ways Justice presents itself in your life.

Notes:

The Hanged Man

4444444444444444444444444

Non-cooperation is a measure of discipline and sacrifice, and it demands respect for the opposite views
— Gandhi

The Hanged Man's trump — is number twelve. The number twelve can be "turned round" to the number twenty-one. This represents The Fool reaching the half way point of The Major Arcana. It can be seen by turning round The Hanged Man card and observing the astonishing resemblance to the dancer pictured in The World (destination card and trump twenty-one). The only difference being that the figure is free in The World with loose sashes, rather than hung up by them.

Twelve encompasses one and two, following on from the prior presences of the masculine Magician and feminine High Priestess in Justice. This thread weaves through an emergence of empowerment from deep contemplation. Twelve also deduces three who is The Empress, the archetypal mother, the gestation period culminating in new life. Twelve initiates another rite of

89

passage. There are twelve months in a year, twelve signs of the zodiac and every twelve years Jupiter finishes one cycle and begins another. So I guess you wonder why I have used the number four (under the title) to represent The Hanged Man? Look at the figure. He is in a shape of a four. Four is representative of a still point, like a chair, or table.

Astrologically — The twelfth sign Pisces rules The Hanged Man, which is hinted at by the foot in suspension, the foot is the body part assigned to Pisces. Pisces is the last sign on the zodiac wheel (Last turn on The Wheel of Fortune). In the first sign of Aries, the focus was on the self. The Fool has now worked through the various stages of evolution and reached ultimate dissolution and merging of self with source. The Hanged Man is governed by Pisces ruling planet Neptune.

Neptune is a mysterious dreamy outer planet in our solar system, therefore a slower and more elusive planet. Neptune captures the deep, receptive, imaginative, unfathomable, unconventional, mystical, sacrificial nature of The Hanged Man.

Tree of Life — The Hanged Man is hung upon the pathway between Geburah (destruction and change) and Hod (intellect, logic and structure).

Symbolism — The most obvious connection is with the sacrifice of Jesus, hung upon the crucifix (Tree of Life). Also to be found is Buddha's Bodhi tree enlightenment, and Norse God Odin's sacrifice on The World Tree, who hung himself upside-down, plunging headfirst into the underworld. This symbolised the initiation/injection of consciousness into the unconscious in order to receive deep nurturing enlightenment and feed it back up to the world, thus initiating a deep and powerful shift of perspective. We also see the yogic tree pose pictured. The hands tied behind his back pictures the element of sacrifice, but as this is all Piscean, it could all be an illusion! The way one leg is crossed behind the other may refer to the Knights Templar and their connection with the Freemasons; they in turn were associated with the Gnostic heretics who insisted on the possibility of a direct inner connection to God available equally to everyone — and this Hanged Man has a very clear halo of holiness around his head. The heresy was persecuted by the Church because such simplicity would turn the world upside-down and there would be no need for priests. There is a paradoxical manner in The Hanged Man. The theme of empowerment and liberation through vision takes an unconventional twist. A picture speaks a thousand words. The Hanged Man is so simple in its design but says so much. Within the simple symbolism there is much symbolism, but it is lost by trying to understand it. Another polarity? A message of truth? We sometimes get so hung up we get stuck and in order to transcend a simple look at the bigger picture is all that's needed. Like the magic eye pictures, softness accesses.

Neutrality/negativity/positivity — Slow natured, the passage of time pictured here maybe the greatest challenge. Surrender to limbo, aware the only thing he can change is his perception. In doing so, he transcends the discomfort of experience and discovers the gifts within. The Hanged Man can picture frustrating delays where we just don't know how to shift out of the situation. The situation often doesn't shift without an inner shift of perspective, going deep within in order to work out what to sacrifice so we can move on. The thing to sacrifice is found usually deep in the sub-conscious, where we find the part of ourselves hung up on something being a particular way.

Bringing The Hanged Man Alive

* Sleep with The Hanged Man under your pillow and note your dreams.

* Write verse.

* Are you or do you know a person who sits on the fence?

* Are you someone who finds decisions hard?

* Embark on a journey of the subconscious through meditation or dream work.

* Research ascended masters such as Jesus, Buddha and Odin (or a more modern archetype such as Gandhi).

* Meditate.

* Give up something.

* Think back to times in your life where all you had the power to do was shift your perspective, how was the outcome?

* Try shifting your perspective on something now and see what happens with the passage of time.

* Write down all the ways The Hanged Man manifests in your life.

Notes:

Death

1313131313

The important thing is this: To be able at any moment to sacrifice what we are for what we could become.
— Charles DuBois

Death's Trump is — number thirteen. Associated with bad luck, this number has the extraordinary power of evoking fear, Friday the thirteenth being the day Judas betrayed Jesus and Judas being the thirteenth guest at The Last Supper. Thirteen moons of the year associated to witchcraft. What we see is a strong Christian fear deeply rooted around Death.

Thirteen deduces to four, the man made structure of The Emperor. Thirteen separates into one — the empowerment present in The Magician, and three, The Empress echoing the promise of new life on the other side. Man-made plans (The Emperor) become so narrow and rigid that it completely stops moving (Four and The Hanged Man). If we do not shift, life comes along disguised as Death and shifts us (The Magician), either kicking or screaming in resistance (the negative side of

The Emperor), or in peaceful surrender (the positive side of The Hanged Man). The outcome is to leave us in an environment bursting full of new nurturing life (The Empress).

Astrologically — The fixed lethal stinging sign of Scorpio rules Death, echoing death as a fixed outcome for all. The deep watery nature of Scorpio acts as a deeply private dark mass, an interior world as deep but even more unfathomable than The Hanged Man. The Hanged Man is non-confrontational but the Plutonic nature of Death plunges to confront. A merciless truth seeker, Death holds the secret recipe for delicious transformation.

Tree of Life — Death is found on the pathway between Tiperath, (beauty, harmony and consciousness) and Netzach (creativity and anarchy).

Symbolism — Rich in its tapestry, Death has priceless gems littered around the landscape for us to discover if we are brave enough to open our eyes and face the:

Grim Reaper — inescapable fate rides high above all the powerless humans, no matter their different positions of worldly man-made power. There are echoes of late medieval paintings of the Dance of Death, connected to the Black Death.

White horse — signifies the intention is pure. The Grim Reaper is your greatest ally disguised. So pure are his intentions that he is only motivated by real love, a love free from ego, free from attachment. A love so deep and true that if he is to be feared and considered unkind to all, then so be it for that is his sacrifice (The Hanged Man).

The horse's reins — show the skulls and crossed bones which became a pirate's flag — but before that they were a symbol of the

Knights Templar and later the Freemasons.

Flag — The white rose on a black background pictures the purity of heart prevailing and transcending and has five petals, referring to the four elements plus spirit.

The King — defeated. Reminding us that worldly status and power no longer mean a thing in the face of Death.

The Priest — nearly as powerless. His faith allowing him to stand before and confront Death, but Death still comes to him. He has a bishop's mitre, showing that even the most powerful priests still bow before Death like the King.

The Child — welcomes Death with flowers, the purity of her heart shines through. Even though she cannot escape death, her lack of knowledge and youthful naivety protects her far more than the King with his powerful identity, or the Priest with his educated faith. From children we can learn so much. Children live for the day; living life through the angel of death teaches us to do the same.

The Two Towers — in the background represent the two pillars pictured in The high Priestess, except here there is no veil present and all is revealed. The veil in-between the two worlds no longer exist.

The Sun — is rising, the dawn of a new day beginning a new life. The light of rebirth is now present at the end of the tunnel.

The flowing river — of change.

Neutrality/positivity/negativity — It is no coincidence that The Fool experiences the lessons of surrender in The Hanged Man before Death. If there ever was a time for those learnings to be tested, it is in Death. Human nature keeps us clinging to what we know and in fear of what we don't. But if we can face up and surrender (paradox) to that which we fear we find ourselves on the other side (Death) stronger, wiser and better for it.

The season of Death is Winter. The old life of the previous cycle dies away in preparation for new life in the spring, a necessary step, without which life cannot continue. No sin is more punishable than resistance. Death is slow natured, we are all living and dying (another paradox). But surrender is the lesson of grace in The Hanged Man. If we hang ourselves upside down and surrender to the experience, our perspective will change. In plunging deep down to the dark night of the soul, we arise reborn, a lot easier and faster. Opening our eyes to the experience, we see the shining beauty of the gems littered around the landscape, and realize in the reflection that the gems are us.

Bringing Death Alive!

* Sleep with Death under your pillow and note your dreams.

* Write verse.

* How do you feel about Death?

* In the West we are not trained well in the rite of Death. Consider reading "The Tibetan book of Living and Dying" for graceful surrender.

* How are you with confronting truths and fears in your life?

* Make a pact to do one thing each day that scares you.

* Consider connection with the other side — mediumship,

astral journeying, channelling, life between life hypnotherapy, working in a hospice etc...

* How are you with change?

* How are you with Winter?

* How are you with age?

* Live by the angel of death in your daily life — this is POWERFUL. Live everyday as if it were your last, no longer taking anything for granted and appreciating all. It heals relationships, balances perspective and reminds us what is important.

* Write down all the ways Death materializes in your life.

Notes:

Temperance

XIV

You wrote to me once, listing the four chief virtues: Wisdom, justice, fortitude and temperance. As I read the list, I knew I had none of them. But I have other virtues, father. Ambition.
— Commodus

Your faults as a son is my failure as a father.
— Marcus Aurelius, from the film *The Gladiator*

Temperance's Trump is — number fourteen, a higher octave of the already magic number seven. Here we see increased magic, spirituality, power and transition. Fourteen also deduces to one, the spark of new life in The Magician. And four — physical matter in The Emperor. As Temperance seems fluid this feels paradoxical but the angel (who itself is androgynous) is combining perfectly the two polarities in life to create total wholeness (healing). Lastly, one and four makes five, reminding us of the spiritual fifth element.

Astrologically — Temperance is Sagittarius, half horse/half man, signifying change and transition. Having gone through death and into rebirth Sagittarius is known as a positive, optimistic, progressive sign that stands for far reaching vision, transition, spiritual vocation, and flexibility.

Tree of Life — Temperance is found on the pathway between Tiperath (beauty, harmony and consciousness) and Yesod (reflection and imagination).

Symbolism — the combination of opposites ascertaining true balance, is a path that requires complete consciousness. The mid path is all things in moderation. Temperance is the fourth virtue. In Temperance, we see the gentle resolute knowing of Strength, the quiet patience of The Hermit and the balanced vision of Justice. Temperance encompasses all four virtues. In Temperance, we see the Greek Goddess Iris who guided the souls of the dead across the river Stix, through the veil to their next plane. Some say she is the only god/goddess to have access to all seven planes, including the underworld. Hence, she is also represented as the seven coloured rainbow.

The Angel — stands one foot on earth, and the other in the sea picturing the mix of two opposites (solid physical matter and the flow of creation). The angel itself appears androgynous hinting at combination of opposites.

Chalices — pictured in nearly all Tarot decks, the angel pours water back and forth between two chalices with perfected ease. Attention never wavers, water never spills. In fact the water is almost always pictured pouring diagonally, which is an impossible transition in itself. Some decks go further by picturing one vessel with the Moon, the other with the Sun, or the elements are represented as one silver and the other gold. The chalices picture the necessary combination of peaceful, balanced emotion for healing and transition. This is yet another repeat of the Tarot's main message, the importance of the soul's journey in combining polarities.

The yellow triangle — represents illuminated spirit within.

The square — matter.

Third eye — indicates clarity and vision shining deep within, represented by the sun shining in the middle of the forehead. This perfectly pictures the powerful enlightenment and far reaching vision of the fully activated third eye. The third eye is also our centre of balance.

The Path — leads to the dawn of a new day; the way to enlightenment is a journey and one to be savoured. This path tells us that we are on the other side as it is the same landscape that is revealed in Death. No longer is the gateway to the other side represented by pillars but two mountains, showing us that the way to enlightenment maybe through the up and down cycle of rebirth.

Neutrality/positivity/negativity — Temperance is more obvious in its neutrality than a lot of other trumps, with its importance placed on balance, consciousness and moderation. It signals to us the ever-important repetitive message that both polarities have a part to play in the journey of enlightenment. Temperance can also indicate the presence of imbalance and quite simply the need for balance.

Bringing Temperance Alive

* Sleep with Temperance under your pillow and note your dreams.

* Write verse.

* Practice stillness.

* Practice balance.

* Practice meditation.

* Practice awareness.

* Practice patience.

* Practice focus.

* Practice perfecting an art.

* Read about the Greek God Iris and the river Stix.

* Read about angels and the seven planes of existence.

* Go on a journey — and savour every moment.

* Connect with a horse.

* Teach something you have perfected — (kind of!).

* Go travelling as a teacher or aid worker.

* Listen to the subtle quiet energies of spirit.

* Study healing or earthbound spirit removal.

* Write down all the ways Temperance manifests itself in your life.

Notes:

Chapter 7

The Fool's Journey — From Maturity to Reincarnation

The Devil

THE DEVIL.

IVIVIVIVIVIV

The unconscious is not just evil by nature, it is also the source of the highest good: not only dark but also light, not only bestial, semi — human, and demonic but superhuman, spiritual, and, in the classical sense of the word, "divine".
— Carl Jung

The Devil's Trump is — number fifteen. Fives in the Tarot (as said before) are spiritual in nature; however they also mark a point of tension before the breakthrough. There are three lots of five in fifteen representing the holistic balance of a person in their mind, body and spirit. Within their holistic balance, they are undergoing chaotic tension.

The Devil shows that dis-ease always starts at the level of the spirit and drips down to the mental/emotional level, finally presenting itself physically. It can manifest as a multitude of mental illness, co-dependence and addiction. Like a shadow, its form is limitless. If you try to squash it somewhere, it just comes up elsewhere. The Devil is a general significant indicator of dis-ease and imbalance in oneself and life. Fifteen deduces to one symbolising the dark side of The Magician, and in five, we see the dark side of The Hierophant. Both indicate masculine trickery, deceit and abuse of power. If we add one and five together, we get six which is the trump number of The Lovers and the number of progression after change (the step on from the Hierophant).

Astrologically — The Devil is Capricorn, a zodiac sign known as narrow-minded, materialistic, pessimistic and in fear of becoming empowered. Capricorn is also ambitious, persistent and determined. Capricorn spends a tremendous amount of energy resisting change because of a deep, subconscious fear of all the things change may bring to light.

The Devil and Capricorn are both ruled by Saturn (see the glyph on The Devil's hand), the sign of Saturn on a hand is said to be the signature of The Devil. As said previously Saturn is known as the major malefic planet, heavy and suppressive in nature, weighing down as the lord of karma and hard taskmaster. This view is one sided. The word Saturn translates as "way shower" and Lucifer translated means light bringer. Saturn/Lucifer may embody energies of fear and control, destruction and hardship, confinement and redemption. But through this comes resilience, strength, discipline and the final illumination of the shadow self, leading to enlightenment, freedom and the ultimate empowerment.

Tree of Life — The Devil is found on the pathway between

Tiperath (consciousness) and Hod (intellect, knowledge and structure).

Symbolism — A slow and heavy card, weighed down with its symbolism of darkness. It is rich in esoteric symbolism representing the shadow side of human nature. Being earth, it is the densest darkest element, gravity tempting Lucifer, the fallen angel.

The Devil — In the stance you can see the shadow sides of The Hierophant and The Magician. Everything is a reversal with The Devil. From the introverted hand gestures of The Hierophant to directing his black magician's wand down to the earth, a move stating the denial of spirit. All that matters is matter. An abomination and denier of spirit, he appears to crush faith or hope. The Devil relies on fear and illusion to keep you unconscious, for in that he can reign.

The Hand Gesture — The Hierophant's hand gesture represents being a channel for God, where as the hand gesture of The Devil is a reversal stating that reality stops here, denying spirit or faith.

The Wand — is black (representing unconsciousness) wand is igniting the man's tail picturing the burning desire of physical passions and the lower self.

The Pentagram — each point stands for an element, air, water, fire earth. At the top point should be the fifth element— spirit. But here it is inverted, once again symbolising that there is nothing above, only below.

The Man and Woman — once again representing the opposite polarities present in the universe. Here we see the repetitive theme of Adam and Eve present earlier in The Lovers, but here the serpent of temptation has come out on top. In Adam and Eve, we see again similarities to The Hierophant by the fact that the picture denotes two people lower than The Devil. Picturing the power yielded over them. Although it seems they are chained to The Devil, the chains are actually loose enough to slip off. It is just their fear and unconsciousness, which gives the illusion such power.

Neutrality/positivity/negativity — The Devil marks a very uncomfortable time for The Fool. Remember the saying 'ignorance is bliss'? When The Devil shows up it signifies the initial stages of awakening, ignorance is weakening and so is bliss. Consciousness is dawning and whatever seemed all right yesterday, no longer is. The shadow side has walked right up to The Fool and presented him with a clear opportunity to wake up. Fear may keep The Fool in resistance, but as they say — there is nothing to fear except fear itself. If that is the case, The Fool's discomfort will be pushed aside and The Devil's reign maintained. Never the less the appearance of The Devil shows a powerful opportunity for freedom and tremendous awakening.

Once consciousness has been experienced (as in Temperance), the ego battles harder to hold on as it falls into the grip of its own tactic (fear). The ego fears annihilation of identity (change). This is where people on the spiritual path can become unstuck, through raising their consciousness the ego also rises. Consciousness always versus unconsciousness. If you raise the light, the dark gets darker. But if we journey through the darkness, celebrating it for the gifts it holds within, we become holistically enlightened. That is why The Devil is also known as The fallen angel Lucifer (Light bringer) as without darkness there cannot be light. What a truly awesome gift that is!

Bringing The Devil to Life!

* Sleep with The Devil under your pillow and note any dreams.

* Write verse.

* Ask yourself if you or anyone you know is resistant to facing the truth in certain situations and why that might be?

* Ask yourself if you or anyone else has any self-destructing habits and why that might be.

* Ask yourself who pushes your buttons and why? Do they represent a repressed shadow of you somehow?

* Consider going through some therapy to illuminate unconscious parts of the mind.

* Ask yourself about your belief systems— what are they, where do they come from, are they healthy?

* Who and what situations in your life would be represented by The Devil?

* What is your relationship to money like?

* Do you have any addictive tendencies?

* What are you afraid of?

* Practice doing one thing that scares you every day.

* Practice waking yourself up from habitual attitudes, behaviours and responses.

* Practice raising your light and working productively with your shadow at the same time.

Notes:

The Tower

XVI

It is a great mystery that though the human heart longs for Truth, in which alone it finds liberation and delight, the first reaction of human beings to Truth is one of hostility and fear!
— Anthony De Mello

The Tower's trump is — number sixteen, an incredibly empowering number. The emotional dilemma of The Lovers (represented in trump six and in The Devil), is resolved in the combination of the progressive six with the decisive action of one (The Magician). Igniting the light, consciousness and will, Adam and Eve have awakened. Add together the one and six and you reach the magical transformative number of seven.

Astrologically — The Tower is ruled by the planet Mars, which indicates the sudden, violent and dramatically explosive power. The Tower is one of the fastest cards in the pack. The consciousness has suddenly awakened and The Devil's chains removed.

Tree of Life — The Tower is found on the pathway between Hod (structure) and Netzach (creativity and anarchy)

Symbolism — The Tower speaks for itself; straightforward and uncomplicated it gets straight to the point. Biblically it relates to the Tower of Babel, which was built for the worship and praise of man instead of God. The old beliefs about being struck by lightning if you upset God, and pride coming before a fall is pictured strongly by The Tower.

The Tower — represents the prison of ignorance and unconsciousness (The Devil).

The lightening strike — the wrath of God, the power of Mars and the strike of enlightenment.

The man and woman falling — Adam and Eve forcibly expelled from their restricted unconscious state.

Neutrality/positivity/negativity — The Tower is one of the most feared and misunderstood cards of The Major Arcana, along with Death and The Devil. Nothing in life is to be feared, only understood. When understanding is reached, amazing transformation occurs. Death is a much slower drawn out process. The Devil is a harder place than The Tower as one is becoming aware they have an uncomfortable process ahead of them. The Tower marks the end of the difficult process, yet many people feel when they have The Tower that the difficulty has only just begun.

Everything has just blown up, and so quickly that they are likely to be in shock.

Yet this process began in their unconsciousness (The Devil). They have gone through the difficult stages of emotional turmoil in the inner self. Even if they feel The Tower has happened to them, their subconscious will have been screaming out for resolution of a situation they have not been happy with. Their prayers will have been answered. Be careful what you wish for and be sure to use your imagination wisely, or it will use you. It is only now we see the external manifestation of the subconscious in The Tower that we see what has been occurring inside The Fool for some time. There is nowhere left to hide it, he has to face it. However, he does have free will. He can still resist, but it would be a futile and painful choice.

The process is pictured perfectly with the lightening striking deep into the inner core of The Tower, causing people to be thrown helplessly out of their confines. But does The Tower look like a nice place to be confined in? Especially now you can see how it represents The Devil? The Crown being knocked from the roof of the Tower and worn by one of the people falling down symbolises earthly power and oppression, destroyed by the power of the storm God.

The lightning actually symbolises enlightenment striking through the crown chakra of a person so they can transcend to consciousness and true freedom, like the Phoenix rising from the ashes.

Bringing The Tower Alive

* Sleep with The Tower and record your dreams — has the subconscious given you a message?

* Write verse.

* Think back over your life, looking at times when The Tower struck — were you in a Devil situation before hand? Was it a blessing in disguise? Did you handle it with resistance or excitement?

* What are you secretly longing for right now?

* Are you repressing that or consciously listening?

* Practice feeling the fear and doing it anyway.

* Break out of repression and restrictions.

* Join a freedom rally.

* Inspire others.

* Live passionately.

* Practice feeling alive

* Read "Feel The Fear and Do It Anyway".

* Practice using the power of your imagination, rather than it using you.

* Write down all the ways The Tower represents itself in your life.

Notes:

The Star

****

Work like you don't need money, Love like you've never been hurt,
And dance like no one's watching.
— Crystal Boyd

The Star's Trump — is number seventeen. The magical transformation of number seven (The Chariot) has been activated in the creative beginning of number one (The Magician). Add one and seven together and you get an infinite supply of energy in the symbol of infinity (Strength).

Astrologically — The Star is ruled by Aquarius representing the humanitarian, visionary and deeply spiritual values present within this card.

Tree of Life — The Star is found on the pathway between Chokmah (creation) and Tiperath (consciousness, beauty and harmony).

Symbolism — in this card is very ancient. The Egyptian links are prominent.

The Ibis Bird — in the tree indicates The Egyptian God of magic and medicine — Thoth.

The Naked Maiden — shows there is nothing to hide. Like Temperance, she pours water from two vessels, but here she pours freely. From one vessel, she pours water onto the land without a care, knowing that supply is infinite. Like Temperance she has one foot on land, the other foot is on the water rather than in it. The slight difference is being in tune with the unconscious, rather than submerged, here everything is becoming whole rather than movement in gain to access by it. Infinity is channelled into physical existence.

The maiden represents the Egyptian Goddess of the sky, Nut. Her father Shu is the God of air. Her mother Tefnut is the Goddess of dew and rain. Her brother is the earth God, Geb. Nut coupled with Geb against the wishes of their grandfather, the Sun God Ra. Ra forced Shu to separate them, declaring that Nut would never bear children on any day of what was then the three hundred and sixty day year. However, Thoth took pity and made it possible for her to bear five children by creating five extra days where she could be with Shu. From that union, came the Egyptian gods and goddesses Osiris, Horus, Set, Isis and Nepthtys.

The Eight Stars — are eight pointed reminding us of the infinite power of real strength abundant in the universe. The large Star above her head is symbolic of the higher self-activation, which occurs when the seven major chakras (the seven smaller stars) are aligned.

Neutrality/negativity/positivity — Here the walls of The Tower no longer exist. The Fool once again finds himself in a world full of infinite possibilities, mirroring his natural state before he undertook the journey. After all The Fool and The Star, do share the same zodiac sign of Aquarius. Common themes between The Fool and The Star are elements of guidance and trust but also ungroundedness. The Tower is no longer there and the world is totally expansive, suddenly we feel the need to hang on to something, anything. This is the challenge of The Star.

The Star is usually a favourite of the Tarot. It is an infinitely beautiful place to be, especially after the confines of The Tower. However, there are just as many tests here that are less obvious than the other cards. The Fool has the world as his oyster, but it would do him well to remember that we only see stars when it is night, when we are gazing up at an infinite, mysterious universe. Have you ever done that and felt dizzy, overwhelmed or lost your footing? Sometimes the infinite expanse can fill us mere mortals with a need to feel safe, to have structure, to be housed. The lack of structure has us running back to The Tower, desperate to rebuild what we had and before you know it, The Fool has reverted to the fear place of The Devil, at the beautiful and crucial time of the possibility of the dream coming true. In The Star, The Fool stares right at the true power of the universe, realizing how little he is. If he can see there is something much grander than him at work, have the faith to let things go and hand them over to the universe his blocks disappear. He gets exactly what he needs, but perhaps not how he expected, it is better. Our limited mortal minds couldn't possibly dream up the same amazing gems that are contained within the cosmos, which is also why The Star can be scary. It's all down to our lack of comprehension and trust.

The Star gives the message of eternal hope, love, healing, understanding and creation. It shows peace after trouble and light after dark. It tells us that as long as we are open to the universe, possibilities for the future are so bright they are limitless. But that can be more challenging than we realize as nothing here is familiar, nothing here has structure. The warning in The Star is that it is only us that can limit ourselves. As long as we are aware of that then nothing can dim the bright blessings of The Star.

Bringing The Star Alive

* Sleep with The Star and record your dreams.

* Record your daydreams too.

* Paint the sky or freestyle your creativity.

* Buy a telescope.

* Study astronomy.

* Study astrology.

* Study Egyptian mythology.

* Study magic.

* Give yourself permission to be free, to love, hope, dream and create.

* Visit Egypt — apparently the stars there shine like nowhere else.

* Ask yourself what you wish for and what you fear — can you see a link?

* Read books on trusting, creating, manifestation and letting go.

* Practice being naked in your truth.

* Dance like no one is watching, unbridled and carefree.

* Practice trusting the universe to give you what you need (rather than a person or thing to give you what you want).

* Write down all the ways The Star manifests in your life.

Notes:

The Moon

XVIII

To explain the unknown by the known is a logical procedure; to explain the known by the unknown is a form of theological lunacy
— David Brooks

The Moon's trump — is number eighteen. The Fool has passed through the magical transformation of seven. He is now ready to use the strength given in eight, to recreate his identity in one.

Astrologically — The Moon is ruled by Pisces showing the sensitive, imaginative, intuitive, ever changeable and somewhat confusing emotional depth of this card.

Tree of Life — The Moon is found on the pathway between Netzach (anarchy, sensitivity and creativity) and Malkuth (the root/ subconscious)

Symbolism — in The Moon pictures what is behind the veil in The High Priestess

Water — submerged in the pool of the sub-conscious.

Crayfish — represents the nature of the subconscious. Arising and descending, never completely emerging. Deja vu, glances of forgotten dreams and sudden insights or flashes that seem out of our control. Crayfish are well-known for being able to purify fresh water by eating any rubbish in it!

The Rocky Path — laid out in front of the Crayfish shows the journey it needs to make from the pool of the subconscious if it is ever to become truly conscious.

Canines — the howling pair represent animistic emotions of a primal nature. In some decks, one is black and the other white, to represent the inner battle within of consciousness and unconsciousness. In Rider-Waite, one is a dog and the other is a fox, symbolising the wild and the tame.

The Two Towers — are from The High Priestess's temple as seen from the other side. But now standing unveiled and naked.

The Moon — represents our sub-conscious, our dreams, psychic experiences, intuition, emotions, balance, hormones and change-ability. The Moon represents everything feminine and all three stages of the woman. The waxing Moon is the maiden, the full is the mother, and the waning is the crone.

Neutrality/positivity/negative — After The Fool has embraced the blessings of The Star he finds himself submerged in the dark waters of the Moon (in contrast to The Star where the maiden's foot rested lightly upon it). Do you recall what was said about how being in an unstructured infinite place of possibilities can be uncomfortable? Here The Moon pictures why. Unable to see clearly, the ground has gone and water surrounds us at night. It is now time to delve deep into our emotions (the water) and feel the way forward. Here is the dark night of the soul. The pace slows right down as we need to tread carefully when we can't see clearly. Unable to see outside himself the only sense The Fool has now is his intuition. He has to feel the way forward, but have you ever been confused as to whether you were fearing something or being intuitive? The Moon is forever changing her form, changing the waters in the pool of the sub-conscious. With that, The Fool's emotions continue to change, resulting in disorientation and confusion. However, this is also the nature of intuition, it is instantaneous, it can't be planned!

The Moon is a very surreal, confusing place to be. Our emotional tide consumes us, vulnerability overcomes us, yet the only way through it is through it. No one can hold back the night. It is only by diving into these deep waters, by experiencing the depths of the sub-conscious that we finally emerge with a strong intuitive ability. We learn what it feels like to know ourselves truly, madly, deeply. The Moon houses the past through its strong magnetic pull, signifying time of necessary reflection. No sane person sets off to climb a mountain in the moonlight. We go to bed, enter the confusing world of dreams and awake to climb when the sun to rises as it always does.

Bringing The Moon Alive

* Sleep with The Moon under your pillow and record your dreams.

* Now keep a dream journal.

* Learn lucid dreaming.

* Learn how to interpret your dreams.

* Reflect.

* Have a past life regression.

* Nurture yourself.

* Have healing.

* Practice feeling.

* Practice allowing yourself to feel confused (trusting The Sun to come up).

* Practice feeling okay with feeling overwhelmed or flooded.

* Practice being — rather than doing.

* Practice being gentle, quiet and observational.

* Develop your intuition (but remember to listen and not necessarily act. Things look very different in daylight, maybe you will need to wait for The Sun).

* Connect your feminine side — whether you are a man or woman.

* Pay homage to your mother/mother's line.

* Meditate.

* How is your relationship to your feelings, creativity and intuition?

* How is your relationship to the past, your mother and

children?

* Do you live by the sea?

* How do you feel about water?

* How do you feel about the night?

* Write down all the ways The Moon manifests itself in your life.

Notes:

The Sun

XIX

There is a fountain of youth: it is your mind, your talents, the creativity you bring to your life and the lives of people you love. When you learn to tap this source, you will truly have defeated age.
— Sophia Loren

The Sun's trump — is number nineteen. The nine represents the spiritual quest we have undertaken nearing an end, (The Hermit) and the one shows activation, illumination and enlightenment (The Magician). Added together we reach ten indicating the successful culmination of a cycle.

Astrologically — The Sun is ruled by none other than the Sun! Supreme ruler of the self The Sun has a double helping of potential making it perhaps the most powerful card in the pack.

Tree of Life — The Sun is found on the pathway between Hod (structure) and Yesod (imagination). On first glance that may not seem right but Hod is home to the number eight (the number of

Strength also ruled by The Sun), and Yesod is home to number nine (The Hermit nearing the end of a cycle).

Symbolism — in The Sun card is clear to see, just like the nature of the card.

The Sun — the almighty power of The Sun bestows on us a confident joyful warmth and exuberance. It ignites our creatively inspired passions and it adorns us with a child-like carefree playfulness.

The child riding bareback on the white horse — stands for a double helping of purity, symbolising an innocent playful return to the inner child riding free through life.

The Wall — is a warning to the child to know its boundaries. Do not get too close to The Sun or it will burn. We can have too much of a good thing!

Neutrality/positivity/negativity — The Fool has emerged from his emotional turbulent and confusing sleep in The Moon, fully awakened in The Sun. He is confident he can see clearly, which means two things, clarity and clairvoyance ("clair" means "clear"). Such a light positive card of instantaneous happenings (the pace has speeded right up due to the ability to see) that it is hard to see a negative. But if The Fool becomes obsessed by The Sun there are dangers. He could become a pleasure seeker, getting addicted or burnt.

Sometimes clouds get in the way and we can feel cut off from our source, but nevertheless, you are connected to the source always. Clouds are temporary, reminding us of the importance of balance and time out. The Sun is always there, even if we can't see it. Here you cannot only know it's there and see it, but feel it radiating through every pore of your being. Enjoy this experience, explore the endless source of creativity it holds, grasp the golden opportunities it bestows like butterflies in the air, and you too will fly that high. Here comes The Sun! Now you can go climb your mountain! The Sun's rays dry up our tears from The Moon, enlighten our vision, activate our clarity and warm our souls.

Bringing The Sun Alive

* Sleep with The Sun under your pillow (if you can!) and record your dreams.

* Go on holiday somewhere sunny.

* Get in touch with your creativity.

* Get in touch with your inner child.

* Allow yourself to play.

* Practice being in the now.

* Practice radiating a healthy optimism.

* Practice turning every negative into a positive.

* Practice smiling at everyone you meet and see what happens!

* Practice being social.

* Allow your light to shine.

* Inspire.

* Express yourself!

* Dance!

Notes:

Judgement

XX

Many that live deserve death. And some that die deserve life. Can you give it to them? Then do not be too eager to deal out death in judgement. For even the very wise cannot see all ends.
— J. R. R Tolkien

Judgement's trump is number twenty — the two signifies how The High Priestess's teachings have been behind this journey all the way. Twenty is a higher octave of ten. The Fool has now completed his second trip around The Wheel. Great understanding and spiritual vision has been reached, ending the separation in duality. Divine unity comes together in the two tens.

Astrologically — Judgement is ruled by Pluto, which illuminates the process of death, birth and rebirth. Remember that Death is also assigned Pluto. Death, Judgement and Pluto are two sided, without Death, you cannot have new life and here you have it. Pluto heralds the end of one phase and beginning of another.

This process is one of shedding the old, wiping the slate clean and welcoming the new.

Tree of Life — is found on the pathway of Hod (intellect) and Malkuth (the root/origin).

Symbolism — in Judgement is mainly Christian, the theme of Judgement day.

Archangel Gabriel — sounds his trumpet; the dead hear the call and rise again. The Fool's consciousness becomes illuminated and the call of new life becomes activated. Where we were once hopelessly numb, we now head the call and resurrect.

The Child — has his back to us for we cannot possibly see what form the new life will take, all we know is we have chosen life and can't help but grow.

The Man and Woman — representing Adam and Eve from the passion of The Lovers and the fear of The Devil, through the initiation of The Tower is now finally awakened and truly resurrected.

The Cross on the Banner — signifies a point of no return, a spiritual crossroads has been reached. A trumpet leads the way over the threshold into new life. The red cross on a white background — the cross of St George, who was immortalized after slaying the dragon.

Neutrality/positivity/negativity — Judgement heralds The Fool to rise up to the challenge and step up to the mark. The similarity to The Wheel of Fortune in the ten does not stop at numerology. The karmic implications here in twenty are twice as high. If The Fool can step up, let go and embrace the new the karmic slate is cleared, new life is bestowed and fast. Instantaneous happenings and instant karma shows the power of Judgement and why the karmic implications are twice as powerful as those in The Wheel. The Fool must make sure he is acting with sound judgement. In fact, Judgement is so powerful that it has the power to speed up all the cards in a spread, as if they too rise to the call. That's how bigger opportunity you have here, it is not one to be ignored.

Bringing Judgement Alive

* Sleep with Judgement under your pillow and record your dreams.

* Write verse.

* Practice trusting your instant hunches.

* Release the old to make way for the new.

* Learn psychic cord cutting.

* Learn to say yes when you want to.

* Embrace opportunity.

* Explore what forgiveness means to you and practice it.

* Do what you are called to do and don't worry about others judgements.

* Learn how to be free.

* Practice allowing yourself the space to be you.

* Practice allowing others to be themselves.

* Become conscious of all the times you have imposed your will on another and why?

* Practice noticing instant karma.

* Read about Angel Gabriel.

* Take up the trumpet — but watch out for any instant karma with neighbours eardrums!

* Make a big decision.

* Say yes! — to life!

* Make a big announcement.

Notes:

The World

XXI

If you do the job in a principled way. With diligence, energy and patience, if you keep yourself free from distraction, and keep the spirit inside of you undamaged, as if you might have to give it back at any moment — if you can embrace this without fear or expectation — can find fulfilment in what you are doing now, as nature intended, and in superhuman truthfulness (every word, every utterance) — then your life will be happy. No one can prevent that.
— Marcus Aurelius

The World's trump is number twenty-one — the intuition and passiveness of The High Priestess in the number two is merging with the empowering activation of The Magician in the one. We can see the two cycles have been completed and we are about to be reborn. The Journey of The Fool is a never-ending evolution of the soul. The Major Arcana is not linear, it's cyclic.

Astrologically — The World is ruled by Saturn, the lord of karma. The World is heavily astrological with the same themes as addressed in The Wheel of Fortune.

Tree of Life — The World is found on the pathway between Yesod (imagination/source) and Malkuth (The root/origin).

Symbolism — in The World embraces all the elements of those before. It is Karmic and heavily astrological.

The Dancer — is The Fool who has mastered all the tasks presented in The Major Arcana and now knows how to move gracefully. Twisting and turning with great ease, flexibility and natural balance. The World always rights itself and finds its own point of natural balance. She dances to the drumbeat of The World through being naturally in harmony with the vibration of creation, also pictured by her nakedness.

The Two Wands — are the pillars previously representing consciousness and unconsciousness. At the beginning, The Wand in The Fool was slung loosely across his shoulder unconscious of its power. We have seen the repetitive themes of the wand, polarities and the need to balance. Here in the World, The Fool has achieved that great natural balance of unity. The Wands are held consciously (both white), with gentle graceful confidence, ease and total trust.

The Laurel Wreath — symbolises arrival, success, completion tied up nicely with red tape! It is evolutionary dear Watson! Graduation from the school of life!

The Four Fixed Astrological Signs — represent the stuff that makes the world go round and the stages the soul has gone through to get here, representing the four turning points, making a whole cycle. Once again, they also remind us of the Gospel-writers.

Neutrality/Positivity/ Negativity — In The World, The Fool responded to the call of Judgement. The tasks that were once hard are now welcomed knowing they only provide opportunity for more success. With this amount of empowerment failure cannot exist, in this we have unity consciousness. The World is one. The Fool has arrived triumphantly at his destination. The World is the most successful card in the Tarot; it is a pat on the back from the universe. It is recognition that you have passed through a whole karmic cycle, which truly is something to celebrate — but not for long.

The World is cyclical and The Fool goes on...

Bringing The World Alive

* Sleep with The World and record your dreams.

* Write verse.

* Travel.

* Reflect on your journey.

* Bend, flex, re-balance, unify.

* Take up Hatha yoga or dance.

* Recycle.

* Practice loving kindness to one and all living things and the planet.

* Do something for the community.

* Start a charity.

* Study the nature of collective consciousness.

* See the connectedness of everything — what you just bought, what you just ate, the long line of where it came from, and the long line of karmic affect.

* Think of something to change The World and put it into action.

* Write down all the ways that The World manifests in your life.

Notes:

Chapter 8

Storytelling

The art of storytelling is the art of reading the Tarot. Learn how to tell stories and your vision and readings will flow. Without it, they will be stagnant. In the previous chapters we looked at how to bring the Major Arcana alive, now we look at how to release them from the static 2D card encasing them and get them mingling with each other.

The best way is to keep a storytelling diary. Every evening tell the story of your day with the Major Arcana. Lay out how many you feel you need to, in a row to express your day.

The art of storytelling is the basis of readings. Reading before perfecting the art of storytelling would be like running before learning how to walk.

Through storytelling, we are learning how to connect with the right side of our brain, the creative and intuitive side. This side has been severely undervalued within society, since school age you have been taught to value the left brain of logic and reason. In storytelling we are coming back to the essence of who we were as a child, the imagination must be liberated!

A common mistake in Tarot is that people lay the cards face down, turning them up and reading them one at a time. But every card impacts all the others and must be read in conjunction. They are not stagnant pictures but energies that flow into each other.

For example, say in a simple three-card spread someone gets The Tower, followed by The Wheel of Fortune, followed by the Sun. This would show a sudden (The Tower) change of events (The Wheel of Fortune) that is likely to be the ending of a karmic cycle (Wheel of Fortune and The Sun) causing a dramatic cleansing (The Tower and The Sun), resulting in a much freer way of life (The Tower and The Sun.) Yet if each card was read separately it would be much harder to see the whole process; not only that but what if the end card was The Devil? You may start reading the cards as if they have got over the worst not seeing that fear pulls them right back to the beginning and in order to avoid going over the same old ground they would need to foster their consciousness. Then when you hit The Devil, it can feel like a brick wall rather than a key to knowing what to do.

Chapter 9

Introduction to the Minor Arcana

The Minor Arcana — Gambler or Tarot Reader?

Ever heard the saying "lucky in cards, unlucky in love" ? Did you know whenever a game of cards is played a reading is also being dealt? What makes it one thing or another is your intent.

The Minor Arcana (minor box of secrets) are what our playing cards are based on. Four suits, from ace right through to King. They represent the outer manifestations of the inner workings (Major Arcana). Remember that The Major Arcana are your major box of secrets, they house the all spiritual why. The Minor Arcana shows us the who, how, when, where and what. In short the Major Arcana are your puppeteers and the Minor Arcana the puppets. So reading with an ordinary deck of cards miss out the all important why's of the Major. The Minor Arcana are really easy to read when two things are understood:

1   What the element (suit) represents
2   What the number represents

So for instance if fire represents action and number one represents beginnings then The Ace of Wands would represent the beginning of action. The Minor Arcana are very easy ... once you know how!

Elements

The Four suits in the Minor Arcana represent the four astrological elements of air, water, fire and earth.

Air — The Swords

Air is the fastest element so stands for thought, which is the fastest, unseen vibration there is. Air is represented by The Swords as they slice through the air. As Swords represent air they are also the astrological air signs Gemini, Libra and Aquarius.

Water — The Cups

Water can be calm and soothing or stormy and threatening, water stands for emotion, represented by the vessel that holds — The Cups. As The Cups are home to water, they also house the astrological water signs of Cancer, Scorpio and Pisces.

Fire — The Wands

Fire is one of the quickest attention grabbing vibrations there is, standing for action. Fire is represented by The Wands, being like the match or old-fashioned torch. As Wands house fire they are also home to the astrological fire signs of Aries, Leo and Sagittarius.

Earth — The Pentacles

Earth is the end result of all that has gone before, the manifestation. Being the slowest most stagnant solid vibration there is, of things we can see and touch. It is represented by the solid gold coin — The Pentacle. The Pentacle has the symbol of the pentagram upon it, one point for each element and one point for the fifth element of spirit, all encompassing. As Pentacles house earth, here we are seeing the home for the astrological earth signs of Taurus, Virgo and Capricorn.

The Numerological Key
— In the Major and Minor are the same.

1 Beginnings: Birth and independence.
2 Joining up: Partnership and relating, balance and

imbalance, stalemate and agreement, unity and separation, harmony and disharmony, indecision and compromise, interdependence and co dependence, polarity and duality, masculine and feminine, yin and yang (two sides to everything).

3 From two comes three: Expansion, birth, growth, instability, change.

4 Stabilising: Structure, law, order, reliability, stuck ruts, boredom.

5 Instability: change, conflict, chaos, breakdown.

6 Breakthrough: moving on, leaving things behind, progression.

7 Endurance: Challenge, persistence, ambition, gathering momentum.

8 Strength: Quest, vision, journey, growth.

9 Penultimate: Nearly there, one step away.

10 Arrival: Endings and beginnings.

So here we go, one to ten, with each. Oh where to start?

Chapter 10

The Swords — The Closest Aspect to Spirit

At the beginning, there was The Sword. Swords represent thought. For anything to come into existence it has to be thought of first. The Swords, like Death, The Devil and The Tower have a feared reputation. But all cards are neutral, encapsulating both the negative and positive. The reputation carried by The Swords shows just how powerful thought is and how much it creates our reality. The secret is to look beyond their startlingly sharp first appearances into the deeper, bigger picture. The Swords house infinity. They are the closest we get to the realm of spirit. Think about it. Those ideas that popped into your mind, where do they come from? We can't see the energy of air (well some of us can). We can't see spirit (well some of us can). But we can all feel the air. We can all feel someone's spirit (whether it is in a body or not). The Sword and the spirit are undoubtedly linked. Spiritual evolution doesn't always come through trials and tribulations, but in a lot of cases the more someone suffered the more they finally became empowered.

Think about the most spiritual people you know. Some may have just been born that way, but my belief is that if they were born that way then they did the hard work in previous incarnations. This time they are like earth walking spirit guides. The Buddhist Bodhisattvas that reach enlightenment but choose to stay behind until we all do. My thoughts turn to the guy who runs the always incessantly busy cafe across from Mysteries. Whenever I go in there, he is smiling ten to the dozen, multi-tasking with his go-go gadget arms, mesmerising the return customers with a personal joke. One day he looked at me and "guessed" correctly what I wanted, I joked with him that he was after my job. His reply:

"I am going to upset you now but I don't believe in it."

"That doesn't upset me," I replied. "I already knew!"

"A friend of mine went to one of you," he said. "They told him the name of the woman he was going to marry. It happened. But only because she planted the seed in his head."

"Exactly!" I said. "But isn't that magic? The power of our thoughts. Take you, you work so hard, always here, always overrun, yet in the four years I have been here I have never seen you without a smile and I have never heard a stressed word cross your lips."

"Yes," he said. "You have to, if you don't it all goes wrong — I know! I lie in bed and think about these things! I have a very good brain!"

Not only does this guy have a very good brain, he has learnt the lesson of The Swords. He has learnt how spirit works. But he sees it as the mind side of the psyche, instead of the psychic.

When I met my husband, he felt I needed someone who knew about Tarot, Astrology and Reiki. I told him I didn't because most people who did were searching for something they hadn't attained (myself included). The reason he didn't know about it was because he already had it. Like the cafe man. These are the Bodhisattvas. Just like the big issue seller you see on the same street corner, come rain or shine, day after day. He always remembers you and greets you with a much more genuine hello than your best friend, even though you never give him any money. Then there is the neighbour who was in and out of psychological institutions and set up a spiritual practice to benefit others. Or the now deeply peaceful monk who previously lost his wife to cancer. The blind man who wears a constant illuminated smile, even though he has never been blessed with the elevating beauty that vision can provide. He doesn't need it, he found it through his inner vision. Take the non-stop dancing deaf person, who has never been lucky enough to hear the beauty of music. He found his own inner music, not reliant on the outside player. Then there's the nurse who previously lost her son to leukaemia and relives it every day in her vocation. And there was her son who suffered intensely for years, never complaining and always loving. Who still walks beside her, sending the living his comforting energy through her.

Do you get the picture? The tougher the times the stronger the opportunity to evolve, and in this way The Swords can be the brightest of blessings. However, if ever there was a test for the reader to empower someone, it is when their clients (or even more challenging — their own) reading has a number of Swords in. The Swords come to see if you really can walk your talk. The talk about knowing that everything that happens to you benefits you somehow. The talk about remaining neutral and seeing the silver lining in every cloud (it is no accident that saying is about air). If you manage to do it there really is no greater feeling. The double-edged sword represents that every opportunity can be viewed as a problem or every problem viewed as an opportunity...

Ace of Swords — Beginnings

Imagination is the beginning of creation. You imagine what you desire, you will what you imagine and at last you create what you will.
— George Bernard Shaw

The manifesting hand from the cloud (spirit) represents opportunity presenting itself. The upright Sword shows the thought in the card is neutral. It can be tipped either way by the surrounding cards. When standing alone, or supported by other cards it signifies clear balanced vision. A vision that soars high above obstruction (the mountains), and reaches spiritual integration through the energy centre of the crown chakra (the crown).

There are differentiations about the droplets pictured, some say it is illumination of the Sun, (inspiration). Some say they represent the Hebrew name for God YHVH, also picturing in-spir-ation (spirit within). Some say they are fallen leaves from the pierced laurel wreath over the crown, signifying the hard times are over and a fresh start presented — if you choose to see it. Remember that every card is connected to the others around. No card is an island. If this meaning of The Ace of Swords is not supported by the other cards, it would be talking about the potential beginning for the above. It would also signify a possible block that needs to be identified in order for it to come into full manifestation...

The Two of Swords — Indecision

Indecision may or may not be my problem.
— Jimmy Buffet

The individualised beginning of one has now grown into two. Twos represent partnership or conflict, inner or outer, opposites or unity, balance or stalemate. In The Two of Swords, the one clear thought has grown into two, causing the clear to become unclear. The challenge is pictured well in The Rider-Waite. The two opposing swords cause her to become stuck by one of the most fluent moving of energies — air/spirit, (tip — deal two extra cards, putting one at the end of each sword to gain exactly what the thoughts are). Through the opposing swords, she has become stuck in her head and out of her heart, disconnected from feeling, as pictured by her arms crossed over her chest. Which also picture the vulnerability and defensiveness caused by disconnection. Vulnerability and defensiveness is another opposing aspect of the same energy.

The Blindfold also has a double meaning. Visibly blind to outer seeing — which she may have done to herself (the ostrich head in the sand syndrome). Her only option is to go deeper into her inner vision, reconnecting her anyway.

The vast amount of water that she has her back to, shows the amount of emotion she is afraid to face, but the waxing face of the moon shows that the tide is going to rise. With the weight of The Swords becoming heavier, her arms grow tired. Eventually if no decision is made, surrender will be inflicted upon her as she falls backwards into the rising tide of her emotions. They say a picture can speak a thousand words and this is one of them. It shows how tiring resistant defensive thought is, not even the hardest can keep that stance forever. It encapsulates perfectly how nothing is to be feared except fear itself. It is only fear that guarantees inevitable materialisation of that which you fear! So what is the saving grace of this card?

The inability to see. The blindfold forces her to go within. Without seeing, she has to feel. Once she feels, the power of resistance is broken. She comes out of her head and into her heart, the arms uncross as she puts down The Swords. She can then remove the blindfold, get up, turn round, face the water, and be free to walk on.

The Three of Swords — Growth

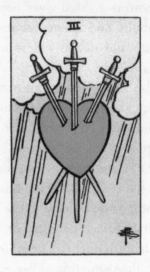

I don't accept the maxim 'there's no gain without pain'. I believe it is possible to develop and grow with joy rather than grief. However, when the pain comes my way, I try to get the most growth out of it.
— Alexa McLaughlin

In The Three of Swords, the two has grown from resistance to feeling. The three is one of the most feeling cards of The Swords. We have gone into the blindfold and into the heart. This card hardly needs any interpretation, three swords piercing the heart. Where has the third come from? Did she turn her sword in on herself? Did she mean to? Or did she fall backwards into the sea, upon another? Did another put the sword in? The Three of Swords represents three pains, three causes, three people. Or that pain manifests holistically (trilogy of mind, body and spirit) if left too long. Painful thoughts cause painful emotions, painful emotions cause painful actions, painful actions cause painful manifestations.

This card is still an improvement on the previous because it shows that the healing process has begun. Often we have to feel to heal, face hard truths and remove thorns in our hearts...

The Four of Swords — Recovery

Blessed are the single-hearted, for they shall enjoy much peace. If you refuse to be hurried and pressed, if you stay your soul on God, nothing can keep you from that clearness of spirit, which is life and peace. In that stillness you will know what his will is.
— Amy Carmichael

In the four, the three has gone through the initial growing pain and is now stabilizing in recovery. Fours in the Tarot symbolise structure and stability, being stuck in confinement or boxed in. Think of a chair or a box, both offer stability. Both are made up of four, whether it be legs or corners. The Four of Swords symbolizes a mental rut or still-point that may or may not be manifesting itself physically. In the image there are three swords pointing to the head, chest and stomach. The holistic message of this card pointing out that anguish in the head, is felt by the emotional centres of the heart and gut, eventually manifesting physically, unless we catch it first. The body's way of making sure we heal is to put us flat on our back, as indicated by the fourth sword.

The stained glass window shows that by being put flat on our back the boxed in mental anguish disappears and spiritual light is in vision. Clearing, illuminating, restoring and showing us the way forward. Whether or not you are feeling mentally blocked or physically unwell, this card stands for retreat. Quite solitude, meditation and reflection are paradoxically the only way forward. The surrounding cards will tell you how well this is being embraced — or not.

Five of Swords — Power Imbalance

Here is a rule to remember in future, when anything tempts you to feel bitter: not "This is misfortune," but "To bear this worthily is good fortune".
— Marcus Aurelius

Fives indicate a point of tension. Things have moved on from the stability of four and have temporarily become unstable. The beginning breakdown of a structure is always the most challenging. Whenever something is dismantled there comes a point when we look at the mess all around and think to ourselves that we may have been better off not starting it at all. If you are like me you will just shove it all back in the cupboard (much to my husband's annoyance). Close the door breathing a sigh of relief as you turn to walk away, and then squeeze your face up tight as you hear the dismantled mess forcing the door back open with an un-ignorable calamity. There is no escaping this point if we are to grow (or want a clean cupboard!)

In The Five of Swords, we come across one of the most intense growing pains which demands to be faced. If you put the mind element (Sword) together with the number five you reach mental instability. Through that we get the breakdown of everything The Sword stands for — intellect, communication, justice, integrity and fairness; leaving inner (and eventually outer) conflict, differences, chaotic heads, disagreements and word battles lying all around in disarray.

This card is double representative in that your client could be signified by the person in the foreground of the image or the people in the background. Your client could be either (or both) the abuser or the abused. Another one of life paradoxes is that victim and abuser energy is the same. It's just expressed in different ways. Like the sexual abuser who plays on his victims sympathy, or the emotional abuse of an unfaithful partner who blames you for letting yourself go. Then there's the mentally abusive friend who drains your emotional energy and accuses you of not caring if you start to change. If you feel like a victim then you are allowing yourself to be treated incorrectly. If this is your relationship to yourself, then it becomes your relationships. The two polarities merge into one. So either way the five of swords is not a healthy situation for anyone to be in (but maybe a necessary step). Retreat or defeat is the only way forward. The surrounding cards will help to define which. Either way the self knowledge that comes out of this situation is vast and will be worth its weight in gold, if we see the silver lining.

The Six of Swords — Moving On

March on. Do not tarry. To go forward is to move toward perfection.
March on, and fear not the thorns, or the sharp stones on life's path.
— Kahlil Gibran

Sixes are an indefinable number. Some interpret them as communicative, others as progressive, charitable or peaceful. But then anything would seem peaceful after the fives. We certainly have got out of the box, gone through the mess and re-stabilized. Now we have more room to move than we had in the four.

The Six of Swords is definitely indicative of mental progress and recovery. We have transcended from the violent defeat of the five and move into refuge. (If any cards represent war torn life and seeking refuge The Five and Six of Swords would picture it perfectly).

In the image, The Swords do not sink the boat, if you removed them the boat would sink. Although the situation is now in the past, the mental and emotional baggage still remains. However, the load is not more than we can bear. Sometimes we have to move on with our baggage or we wouldn't move on at all.

The water is choppy on the nearest side. We are moving out of stormy waters into calmer ones. Generally, this card denotes that we are on the right path and moving forward. Even though swords represent thoughts, sometimes The Six of Swords can show actual journeys over water. If this is the case, it will be a manifestation from the decision to choose different thoughts in order to progress through choppy emotions. The surrounding cards will help you see whether the progress is just in the mind, or whether it has ended in a physical journey. Either way it is always the decision to move to a better place internally. How smooth that is also depends on the surrounding cards.

Seven of Swords — Endurance

I've learned to trust myself, to listen to truth, to not be afraid of it and to not try and hide it.
— Sarah Mclachlan

Sevens denote a time for perseverance, a testing period. It may look more negative than it is. Remember seven is also the magic number. It's the number of work going on behind the scenes. When it is hard to see that things may just pay off it could be quite easy to give up. In The Seven of Swords, the test is mental and takes many forms. From needing to play your cards close to your chest and using your intellect to overcome opposition, to stark warnings of trust issues. Possible outside manipulation abounds, and of course at the centre of that is self-deception. The main theme is truth and how it is being bent. All can be seen by looking at the man making off with The Swords. His body twisted, facing two directions at once, completely out of alignment and balance. The surrounding cards will shed light on whether bending the truth is necessary for the good of all, or underhanded. Either way can bent truth really be aligned for the highest good? Perhaps the need to face up to the truth within yourself or your environment is the true test of endurance? This card represents challenge of intellect, issues of trust, secrecy, deception, flexibility and adaptability...

Eight of Swords — Empowerment

If you are distressed by anything external, the pain is not due to the thing itself, but to your estimate of it; and this you have the power to revoke at any moment.
— Marcus Aurelius

Eights in the Tarot represent strength. After deceiving ourselves through The Seven of Swords, we have found ourselves in what looks like a disempowering situation. But as ever with the Tarot, we have the power of polarity. From ultra disempowerment we become ultra empowered. If ever there was a picture denoting victim-hood and martyrdom this would be it. So how do we empower ourselves in such a situation? Surely, a victim is a victim of outside forces? If that is what you think, go back and read from The Five of Swords again. The number six can be seen as a form of charity. The number seven a test of endurance. The hard work not to revert begins in The Eight of Swords. A typical example is of the battered partner that finally breaks away, but once in refuge their partner bombards them with seemingly heart-felt pleas and perhaps real apologies. The thought comes in that perhaps this time they will change, perhaps they finally mean it. Next thing they know they are back in The Five of Swords having to work through the six and seven just to get back to where they were. This is a typical example of life's lessons coming round harder and harder until we finally get it, find the strength (eight) and move on (to the nine).

Looking at the card we clearly see that the lady is exiled, cut off from what appears to be a source of nurture and support (the castle). She looks bound, but she could walk forward. She cannot go back. Once again, she is blindfolded. Her only sense is feeling. Feeling is the only way through this. When we are strongly attached to someone or something, we may allow ourselves to be treated less than fairly. But there will come a point when we have to face the reality of the situation. Our thoughts and emotions will not let us continue this way indefinitely. Few people reach this point easily; others need a close shave death call. Some seem like they need lifetimes.

I can easily recognize the client who is stuck in the pattern of the not-so-merry-go-round of The Five to The Nine of Swords. It can feel soul — destroying, like there is no reaching them. I used to find that really hard, until I realized that it was only my ego wanting me to be the one to release them. Gosh! Can we eat, breath, love or sleep for another? So why could we end another's suffering? What we can do is drop a pebble in their water, sending ripples of wake up. The eventual wake up will be the result of many other pebbles also landing in the pool. It is the collectivity that does it. It may appear to us that someone got it really quickly and someone else didn't or hasn't. All that does is show you whether you were one of the first or last pebbles...

Nine of Swords — Exasperation

Where does one go from a world of insanity? Somewhere on the other side of despair.
— T.S Eliot

Nines in the Tarot symbolise the near completion of a cycle. This can be a time of pleasure or of pain. Here in The Nine of Swords we near the end of the most gruelling spiritual initiation. In the previous trump, I spoke of the not-so-merry-go-round of the five to The Nine of Swords. Notice I did not include The Ten of

Swords.

In a way, The Nine of Swords is a more challenging time than the ten. In ten, we reach completion. In The Nine of Swords, the mental pressure is still growing. Dear me! No wonder we sometimes feel it's easier to stay in the five! What must we do? Clear the mess in the five. Ask for charity in the six. Look at how we deceive ourselves in the seven. Face issues of victimhood and abuse in the eight, and if we finally find the strength to embrace freedom, we are rewarded with the nine! Is this what freedom looks like? What type of reward is that? Here we have nearly got there, we aren't there yet. The realisation is dawning of how thoughts create emotions, emotions create actions, actions create re-actions, it makes our environment. When the threatening situation and/or person has gone we realize how we got ourselves there in the first place. From that we reach the ultimate depth of victim mentality, the self — torture of self-pity. If ever there was a card to denote despair, it is this one.

The figure sat up in bed shows disturbed sleep. The Swords through the upper chakras show the emotional, mental and spiritual pain. Pointing towards the person it shows their own self punishment. But The Swords don't actually cause any harm. Telling how it is not so much the outside environment, rather their perception of it. The strength of thought is building mountains out of molehills. Running wild, it creates stress, tension and anxiety, mental imbalance leading to sleeplessness, and attacks of the mind/psyche. Psyche is a double meaning word also meaning soul. So here we see the a form of psychic attack that the soul inflicts upon itself. It no longer has anyone to blame. A painful thought is always attached to blame. The soul is moving from blaming others to blaming itself, soon it will be through with that too. This is the blessing of The Nine of Swords...

Ten of Swords — Clearance

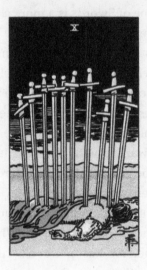

Lay down your sweet and weary head, night is falling, you have come to journey's end ...
Sleep now, and dream of the ones who came before, they are calling, from across the distant shore.
Why do you weep? What are these tears upon your face? Soon you will see, all of your fears will pass away...
— Into The West — Howard Shore and Annie Lennox

Tens in the Tarot represent completion. In The Ten of Swords the soul has realized that the only thing responsible for its pain is it's thoughts. Realization has happened. The aha moment, that no one is responsible for our inner conflict but ourselves. That all we need to do to change our lives is to change the thought. Exhausted through anguish, at the end of despair the only way left is transcendence. Too tired to struggle our ego finally surrenders.

You may be looking at the card, thinking it hardly denotes a time of celebration! You may be muttering to yourself that The Ten of Swords is meant to be one of the worst cards to receive.

But what you are looking at is the end of the lower self. It's not you with ten swords in your back. It's the end of that little devil sat on your shoulder, whispering the not so sweet every-things in your ear. Now how do you feel? Liberated? Reborn afresh at the end of pain and beginning of true freedom? See the new day dawning in the background? Is it an accident that the darkest hour is always before the dawn? This is where the spiritual initiation is completed.

Positivity/negativity/neutrality of The Swords

As mentioned earlier, The Swords come along to see if you are really walking your talk. Are you really able to see how everything in life benefits you? Can you see the incredible gift in The Swords? Out of restriction comes strength, out of despair comes freedom and out of victim hood comes empowerment.

The Swords show us that we are in control of our life. No one else has the control button. The Swords woke us from illusion, pointed out the self-destruct buttons and showed us the ones marked empowerment. Empowerment is different to power. Power denotes control. Control is part of the lower self that was annihilated in The Ten of Swords.

Control implies having power over someone else. Lording it over someone, the same game as giving our power away. It is no longer in us; we are no longer in balance. We came out of our centre the minute we lorded it over. The victim/abuser energy proceeds in both loud lording and quiet manipulation. The leakage of power twists, turns and strangles the other. But only if they too, are not in balance.

We cannot empower another and disempower ourselves. A typical example is of the long-term couple who are no longer in love. They stay with the other as they don't want to voice it and risk hurting the other. Yet they both feel that way. Several years down the line, one of them finally pops. The break up happens and months later, both are incredibly happy with new loves. They wonder why they didn't do it before. Can you think of anymore?

Working with The Swords

- Write about a chapter in your life that felt like The Swords, and assign each step one of The Sword cards. What did you learn? (Or have you learnt from looking at it this way?)
- Is there an area in your life now that feels like The Swords? It could be in your work, your home, your friendships, or your mind, heart or body. Where are you at with it? Give it a Sword card. Where were you at with it a month ago? Two months ago? Three months ago? Are you going backwards and forwards? Keep a monthly diary. A month from today come back and see, have you moved forwards or backwards? Keep in mind that sometimes we have to go backwards to go forwards. Remember not to fall into the blame game (of yourself or others)...

Chapter 11

The Cups — The Power of Emotion

The next step on from The Swords is The Cups. From thoughts (Swords) we get emotion (Cups). Water is emotion, that's why we cry when we are overcome by it. The Cup is the vessel to contain it. Water can be stagnant, flow forwards fast, or drip backwards slowly.

Cups are strongly associated with love. When people think of The Cups it conjures up lovely times in their minds, but love is only one emotion and one that has the all-powerful trigger for many more. Emotions can be fulfilling or soul destroying. Peace, love, joy, happiness and gratitude fulfil the soul. Whereas anger, grief, jealousy, depression, regret, despair and sadness, all possess the power to be soul destroying. Through that journey, do we get to true happiness, happiness, which is no longer dependent on outside circumstance? The Cups are a much loved Tarot suit, and I am just playing devil's advocate. On the whole they do seem much more-happy-go-lucky than the hard work of the swords. But The Swords don't make you work for nothing and the blessings are mixed in every suit. The Cups could be seen as how Dolly Parton once described love...

"The way I see it is if you want the rainbow you have to put up with the rain"...

I am not trying to put a dampener on The Cups. I am just trying to show you that every element has a polarity and that The Cups really are no more beneficial than The Swords, Wands or Pentacles. It is incredibly important to become neutral to whatever cards come up. That way you will see the gifts whatever, and there will be no such thing as a good or bad reading. All of them will have equal power for healing and empowerment.

I am presenting The Cups after The Swords because thought is the absolute beginning of anything. The next step is emotion, which is the embodied reaction to thought...

The Ace of Cups — Emotional Activation

You split me and tore me open.

— Rumi

In The Ace of Cups, we are at the absolute beginning of emotion. The thoughts from The Swords have produced a heart-felt reaction. The Swords have produced an opening. See The Cup being presented from spirit, overflowing with emotion (remember The Cups are hearts). And the blessing of peace from the dove. This definitely is far from an empty experience; this is true heart-felt fulfilment.

The Ace of Cups signifies arrival of an incredibly emotionally satisfying time. This may be the start of an important new friendship or relationship, the start of a career you love, the birth of a longed for baby, or perhaps just an inner arrival of spiritual love. Not that there should be a "just" about that! Inner arrival of this fulfilment shows an incredibly beautiful place that does not rely on external events. Whatever the manifestation (surrounding cards will help to interpret) this is very spiritual in its essence. The difference between the spirituality in The Swords and The Cups is that here we are connected to the heart rather than the head. True happiness overflows from within. Remember that all the cards are aspected by the cards before and after, but whatever the interpretation the main issue here is emotional and spiritual fulfilment...

The Two of Cups — Emotional Partnership

I knew you as I knew myself.
— Rumi

In The Two of Cups, the individual start of emotion has grown. The most obvious formation is a romantic partnership. Although this is certainly one of the strongest cards for denoting such, it is only one interpretation. The positive side of the twos are harmony, connection, understanding, balance, co-operation, commitment, partnership, and relationship. As two is dual, the negative is a reversal. The positive face of The of Two of Cups would stand for balanced, committed emotion. An all important "in it together" union, in which you resonate instantly. The underlying message here is of a deep soul connection. One that can take many forms from friends to family and romantic partners. Most of all this card stands for soul mates.

Soul mates are usually thought of as the person we long to find and will spend the rest of our lives within blissful happiness. While this may be, soul mates take many forms. The one thing all soul mates have in common is commitment to the soul contract above and beyond all else. It is in the name soul mate. In the Rider-Waite, this is pictured by Caduceus growing out of their pledge, signifying a toast to evolution. This activation may take the form of an incredibly harmonious or an incredibly painful relationship (twos house duality).

Healing can sometimes be a beautifully peaceful experience. At other times, it's a turbulent journey, just like the sea (we are dealing with water). Whatever the external appearances this is a deeply important relationship where both of you have committed to the growth of each other through an eternal bond of true love. True love is committed to your healing and evolution, to your highest good. This may not always be what your conscious self wants. If it is, you will be experiencing the best possible relationship. If things feel tough and painful then take comfort in the fact that you are working out of pure soul love for each other, even if it does not look or feel like it.

Being prepared to be hated by the one you love can sometimes be the deepest expression of love (whether the soul is conscious of the process or not), one where the other acts for your higher good (even though it may seem that their behaviour is appalling) no matter what you want or think of them. Take a love relationship, one where one of the partners pushes the other's buttons around forgiveness, all aspects of it. One is always putting the other in a situation where forgiveness becomes an issue. The other finds it really hard to forgive. They don't know how to do it. They can't do it. They break up. They get back together when the other decides to try. But still they haven't done it. They dig at their partner, until the break up happens again. Then they become truly sorry and the relationship gets back on. Until the partner who pushed it in the first place pushes it again. Then the other believes they should have never forgiven them in the first place. The relationship breaks down again. Finally, the other thinks they have forgiven them and goes to tell the other, but the one who pushed it no longer cares — this then pushes the other's buttons once again! "I have finally truly forgiven them and they don't care a hoot", they think. But if they had truly forgiven then it wouldn't matter that their partner doesn't seem to care.

In this way, they are both still helping each other with their evolution. It is showing the one who pushed it that if they feel like they need to be forgiven they will keep doing things in order to be forgiven. Perhaps they need to forgive themselves for something deep down. In the other case, it shows how if we make another responsible for our happiness we will never reach inner balance. This is the so-called negative side of The Two of Cups. What can feel like an intensely frustrating connection. Nevertheless, you will have made a soul contract before you came here to help each other's souls evolve, and you will have been prepared to be hated by the one you love in order to serve each other's highest good. Now that is true soul love.

The Two of Cups can of course also talk about meeting your life partner, the positive side of easy karma. Karma either binds us together or acts as something in between us. The most frustrating side of The Two of Cups is when someone has met a soul mate and mistaken the overpowering emotion as a sign that they must be together. Yet something unworkable is between them, stopping them from completely coming together. This is karma. The souls know they need to work through this, but they also sense that if they do, there may be nothing keeping them together anymore. So unconsciously, they resist working through the contract in the fear of it ending. Of course, sometimes we can work through it and come together. Or at other times the karma is so good you just know it's right, flowing, harmonious in the unity.

The Two of Cups comes up for meeting the one, or meeting a mate of your soul, not necessarily your life-mate. However, it always represents activations of soul contracts and emotional karma.

The Three of Cups — Emotional Highs

You're a happy fellow, for you'll give happiness and joy to many other people.
There is nothing better or greater than that.
— Ludwig van Beethoven

In the three, the soul has grown past the heart-felt cosiness of the two into emotional expansion. This can take many forms. The fruit that was conceived between the two has become ripe to bursting point. This could literally mean a child or another type of creative baby. Something is coming to fruition from the union. Perhaps your relationship has taken in another partner, welcome of not. Whether it is in romance, friendship, or family the stability has gone. Things have reached a place of change, whilst this can be a hugely exhilarating time; it is also one of adjustment and instability, a high and giddy time for the soul and intensely emotional.

The Four of Cups — Emotional Stillness

Not everything that is faced can be changed, but nothing can be changed until it is faced.
— James Baldwin

After the high and giddy time of the three, the next stage for the soul is to land. As four represents stability and The Cups represent emotions, here we are seeing a quiet period of recuperation, healing, retreat and reflection. Of course, the soul can fight this or not. It may be seen as welcome, or inflicted upon. There may be resistance towards being in such a still point. There may be things a person does not want to feel that we can only feel when we are still. They may fight it by feeling stuck, frustrated and bored. The ecstatic dizzy heights are gone. Maybe that great opportunity in The Three of Cups wasn't as fulfilling as you thought. The soul can reflect or react.

In reaction, the soul feels stuck in a rut. Lethargy sets in as it sinks ever deeper into the downward self-pity spiral. Unable to see the exit, because it isn't actually looking for it. All that is in our attention is the dissatisfaction of what we have. Rider-Waite pictures this so well with the hand (opportunity) offering a cup (emotional fulfilment) from the cloud (spirit/thought/air). Once again hinting how our thoughts create our emotions and so forth. But the person is much too much in his lower self to (want to) see...

The Five of Cups — Emotional Lows

...every time there are losses there are choices to be made. You choose to live your losses as passages to anger, blame, hatred, depression and resentment, or you choose to let these losses be passages to something new, something wider, and deeper.
— Henri Nouwen

Remember, fives are a point of tension before breaking through to the other side. How much tension does water have? It is not hard like a Sword, Wand or Pentacle. How can water have tension?

Let's imagine being stood under tarpaulin. Underneath we are dry even though it has rained day and night for a long time. Perhaps forty days and forty nights as represented by the four where the soul created a quiet, still place for self-reflection or self pity. It only saw what it had, not what it could have.

Here in the five the soul has moved its emotional attachments (the three cups from the card before) under the tarpaulin of protection. But still the rain comes. Until one day, the tension in the tarpaulin can no longer withstand. The water (emotion) engulfs the once resistant soul and in doing so, the cups are knocked over. Anything that was carefully contained has disintegrated in a moment.

Rider-Waite pictures this perfectly especially as the liquid is red, the colour of warning, red wine, toxicity, or bloodshed. What was once a cherished life source became contained, stagnant and contaminated. The figure, completely immersed in emotional loss has to accept and grieve. As the emotional intensity increases, spirit increases the signs of new life. In the image what was one offering (Cup) in The Three of Cups is now two. Still the figure does not yet see them. Never the less they are there. This is the last stage before moving on...

The Six of Cups — Nostalgia

Everyone seems to think yesterday was better than today. I don't think it was, and I would advise you not to wait ten years before admitting today was great. If you're hung up on nostalgia, pretend today is yesterday and just go out and have one hell of a time.
— Art Buchwald

Except The Cups aren't that great at moving on! Six mark progression but whereas thoughts (Swords), actions (Wands) and things (Pentacles) all change relatively easily. Water dwells deeply. The heart of the soul has been broken. Often we associate love with pain. The more pain we feel, the more we feel we loved something or someone. It's as if we need to prove our love through a measure of pain. The Cups embody that to the core. Never the less progress is still here. The Cups need to dwell to move forward. They need to go and fall right through the bottom to get to the other side. Consequently, the soul may feel that the bottom has fallen out of their world and they just want to be on the other side. The soul's journey of progression in The Six of Cups can be measured by the way the memories feel. If the feelings still bring tears then the soul is closer to the five and still in the early stages, but sooner or later the sweetness and smiles happen along with the progression.

Rider-Waite pictures a sweet childhood scene, but not all childhoods are sweet. Perhaps also in this card there is a touch of Hansel and Gretel. Our desires and emotions play tricks on us, distorting how things truly are, romanticising about the past through rose-tinted glasses. So even though the six is about moving on, in The Six of Cups the soul needs to go back to know whether they have rose-tinted glasses on or not. A return of past memories (from this life or others), perhaps leading to a physical trip down memory lane...

The Seven of Cups — Confusion

Truth emerges more readily from error than confusion
— Sir Francis Bacon

Sevens represent perseverance. In The Seven of Cups, the soul's challenge is to overcome the tricks we saw in the six. Rider-Waite pictures this perfectly. All these cups! Yet they have an ethereal "are they real?" feel to them. If I reach out and grab one, will it disappear? Will I have made the wrong choice and it will be too late to have a second? Is it true that too much choice is just as challenging as too little? Or is that when we are confused it's for a good reason? Perhaps it's not quite right to make any final decisions yet? Perhaps if we wait the illusions will drop away we will be left with the truth? Or perhaps we are giving into fear? In the card itself, you can see the figure looking at a smokescreen, the fog of confusion. Created by his own imagination. We must use our imagination, or it will use us. In today's society we often put down the imagination by saying "it's just my imagination"! Just? Did you know that the imagination is stronger than the will? Don't think of the colour pink. You are thinking pink aren't you? Even though the will said don't! Do think of the colour green. See — whether I tell you too or not does not matter!

The strength of imagination has created a block so thick. Where did this come from? The imagination sprung from the deep well of sub-conscious and in there was fear. Cries of "I don't know what to do, I am confused" mean the same thing as "I'm scared". It could be that the drama has been created to shield the fear of moving on. It may be a subconscious act of The Six of Cups having one last almighty try at keeping us stuck. Or it may be that we have successfully passed through the five and six and our new life is bursting with potential and opportunity. So which is it? Look at the surrounding cards and listen to your intuition. Like all polarities in the Tarot, there is a thin line. The Seven of Cups may urge you not to rush into making a decision, but like anything there comes a time when we have to move on, or fear turns into self sabotage...

The Eight of Cups — Empowerment

Authentic empowerment is the knowing that you are on purpose, doing God's work, peacefully and harmoniously.
— Dr Wayne Dyer

In The Eight of Cups, the soul has come to a conclusion. It has found the inner strength to remove the rose tinted glasses of the six, moving through the smokescreen of the seven. The soul has woken up to the fact that staying confused only makes a decision for things to stay the same. Now the situation is seen for what it truly is. In doing so it assesses accordingly and realises that something inside has been restless and unfulfilled. We realize that we were confused in the seven because it wasn't quite right. For the first time in The Cups, the ability to move on from the old is found. Now truly able to leave behind what we once had, knowing that is the only way tomorrow will be a better day. The soul has made a breakthrough. The new life although unknown, is embraced. As you can see in the Rider-Waite the seven cups leave a gap, something is still missing. The figure supporting itself with the staff, knows it has to find the inner strength to move on. Because we are in the realm of emotions with The Cups, it is more likely that someone is leaving emotionally and not necessarily physically (dependent on other cards and feelings you get)...

Nine of Cups — Fulfilment

Only those who have learned the power of sincere and selfless contribution experience life's deepest joy: true fulfilment.
— Tony Robbins

Nines represent near completion. Yet in The Nine of Cups, it looks as if completion has taken place. The figure has arrived, possessing all the cups, looking very happy, no loss or quest to be seen. But with The Cups we have one more step to go. What good is love if not for connection and unity?

But can we really, truly love if we have not yet learnt to love ourselves?

The Nine of Cups pictures the complete soul, the one who has found the other half within. The restless quest has come to an end and arrived in a place of self worth and love. The soul has gone through the first stirrings of intense emotions in the ace, into the commitment of the two. Out of commitment came desire and temptation in the three, into emotional lethargy within the four, and loss in the five. Enter nostalgia in the six and dis-empowerment in the seven. Leading to realization in the eight and now into self-fulfilment in the nine. The arrival of true happiness is to make ourselves happy. It is only us that truly knows what goes on inside of us and what our deepest needs are. The illusion of someone else making us happy fell away with the rose-tinted glasses, but rather than disillusioned, we now feel totally emotionally empowered. In The Nine of Cups the insight is realised and all that's left is to share what has been found and in doing so we reach completion.

The Ten of Cups — Harmony

He who lives in harmony with himself, lives in harmony with the universe.
— Marcus Aurelius

The Ten of Cups represents the true arrival point of The Cups.

The Cups need others to drink from it or it has no purpose. Not only can they share their love and sustain others with it, but sharing also sustains them, not in a giving to receive manner, but in the true joy of overwhelming love and generosity. A person brimming with love and no one to share it with is a sad thing indeed, and that would eventually happen to the soul if it stayed in the nine. In The Ten of Cups, we have found our other whole, rather than our other half. Like attracts like. If your feelings or the surrounding cards tell you otherwise then there could be trouble in paradise, but nevertheless, the soul is getting there.

Positivity/negativity/neutrality of The Cups

I wonder now you have gone through the soul's journey in both The Swords and The Cups, if you are beginning to see the trials and tribulations in both. In The Swords, we have the experience of mental torture, but in the end we arrive back round at the same clarity and liberation of the ace, only all the more spiritually aligned and evolved for it. Similarly, in The Cups we have emotional torture, but in the end we arrive back round at the same complete and utter happiness of the ace. Only all the more deep and true for it. Perhaps you can start to see how The Swords are only different in their element. Rather than being the two opposites of supposed blessings (Cups) and supposed curses (Swords)?

Working with The Cups
Write about a chapter in your life that felt like The Cups, and assign each step one of The Cup cards. What did you learn? (Or, have you learnt from looking at it this way?)

Is there an area in your life now that feels like The Cups? It could be in your work, your home, your friendships, relationships, or your mind, heart or body. Where are you at with it? Give it a Cup card. Where were you at with it a month ago? Two months ago? Three months ago? Are you going backwards and forwards? Keep a monthly diary. A month from today come back and see, have you moved forwards or backwards? Keep in mind that sometimes we have to go backwards to go forwards. Remember not to fall into the blame game (of yourself or others)...

Chapter 12

The Wands — The Magic of Creation

Welcome to The Wands. The first two suits of The Swords and The Cups are of a feminine/passive/yin nature. In The Wands, we swing into the masculine/active/yang nature. The Wands are the point where the inner workings start to show themselves externally. After the thought process of The Swords, we felt our emotions in The Cups. The combination of thought (Swords) and emotion (Cups) brings inspiration and passion, creating motivation and action in The Wands. Wands represent fire; just think of a match, a log or an old-fashioned torch. Fire represents all consuming passion, exhilaration, inspiration, courage, motivation, transformation, light and of course eventual burnout. Just like the spread of fire, The Wands hold some of the fastest cards in the pack as well as some of the most consuming...

The Ace of Wands — Inspiration

So show a little inspiration, show a little spark. Show the world a little act when you show it your heart.
We've got two lives—one we're given, and the other one we make, and the world won't stop, and actions speak louder. Listen to your heart.
— Mary-Chapin Carpenter

In The Ace of Wands our emotional fulfilment found in The Cups can no longer be contained. The flowing feelings spill forth into inspirational creativity. Igniting action and sparking motivation. Creating innovation leading to initiation. Inducing fertility, producing passion, creating desire and a strong willed manifestation. If ever there was a clear analogy for The Ace of Wands it would be the match. That strike of ignition. Promise of new life is signified by the leaves sprouting from The Wand. The inspiration is shown by the hand of spirit (cloud) eureka!

The Two of Wands — Deliberation

In the conduct of life we make use of deliberation to justify ourselves in doing what we want to do.
— William Somerset Maugham

In The Two of Wands, that instantly fast spark of inspiration has slowed right down by dividing or multiplying in two. The figure comes to a standstill whilst he works out the best way forward. Remember in twos we see partnership, deliberating, projections, and dilemmas. Here the dilemma is of what action to take next. The latter belonging perfectly to The Two (dilemma) of Wands (action). Because The Wands are active, we have fast forwarded to a halt already!

In one hand, the figure holds The Wand of familiar territory with all its security, but its restrictions as represented by the wall. Then there is The Wand of promise, a new life beckoning the soul forward with a magnetic pull of discovery as represented by the world. The Wands are fast and impulsive, it will be hard for the soul to resist this pull, but fear of the unknown can temporarily paralyse. The Two of Cups is very stationary for a Wand card.

The Wands are very quick and already in The Two of Wands, the soul has nearly reached the point of no return. One more step (over the very low wall) and all will change...

The Three of Wands — Expansion

Vision — it reaches beyond the thing that is, into the conception of what can be. Imagination gives you the picture. Vision gives you the impulse to make the picture your own.
— Robert Collier

In The Three of Wands, the soul has embraced action and overcome restriction (stepped over the wall), but still we are at a very slow pace for The Wands. Fear of the unknown still exists even though the soul is in the process of opening (pictured by the widened placement of The Wands). The figure has set his ships out to sail, acting as antennae testing the waters. The figure stands safe on the edge of dry land. The soul knows it has done all it can and now has to wait for his ships to come in. The Three of Wands pictures good foresight, a quality of The Wands. Fire is visual, when the Sun is up, we can see clearly. Subsequently the

Wands are clairvoyants (clear-seers). So here, we also see qualities of premonition, and prediction.

The Four of Wands — Destination

The future is not a result of choices among alternative paths offered by the present, but a place that is created — created first in the mind and will, created next in activity. The future is not some place we are going to, but one we are creating. The paths are not to be found, but made, and the activity of making them, changes both the maker and the destination

— John Schaar

The soul's ship came in and transported him safely to his present place of being. The past actions are now being consolidated and celebrated. They have been actions of improvement, achievement, success and glory. And quickly too of course! This is like a ten but we are only at four! This is but a pause in the life of The Wands. The fire here is really well contained. Like the hearth producing a beautifully warming homely feel, but restless, impulsive, inspired Wands need to create. Fours may signify boredom, but they don't get a chance in The Wands! The Wands recharge in the fire of the four and are out of there as soon as they are reignited.

The Five of Wands — Conflict

The harder the conflict, the more glorious the triumph. What we obtain too cheap, we esteem to lightly; it is dearness only that gives everything its value. I love the man that can smile in trouble, that can gather strength from distress and grow.
— Thomas Paine

And so the soul arrives at the five. In The Five of Wands, we see the breakdown of structure created in the four. I told you Wands were fast and restless! Creation needs to destroy if it is to keep creating. The five is a point of tension. Tension in The Wands is expressed as friction. Friction is also a source of passion (do I have to explain?) passion becomes uncontrollable sometimes spilling over into creation and destruction (do I really have to explain?) As I said before The Wands are masculine, potent and phallic! So here, we have change for change sake. You didn't really think The Wands could stay in the lovely environment of the four for long did you? No, it has too many seeds to sow! If a fire is left, does it stay in one place? Well if you did think that, you will be left crying in that hanky, hopefully it wasn't used earlier! The Five of Wands denotes destruction, change, and conflict. The conflict is most definitely within, but as The Wands are expressive and yang, this conflict will be expressed dramatically and in some perverse way probably even enjoyed. Do not get The Five of Wands confused with the deliberate troublemaker; fire never deliberately destroys, just like it never deliberately warms. It just is.

The nature of the Wand cannot help but blaze. In the card, we see five figures hitting each other with their Wands. It's a testosterone brawl! Working together constructively is a no-no. Exhausting their hotheaded excesses through impulsive reaction, is a yes-yes. The Five of Wands is attention seeking, loud, destructive and scattered. Just like fire itself. The Five of Wands is almost impossible to contain and redirect. Nevertheless, with the right approach we can harness our passions for beneficial outcome...

The Six of Wands — Victory

Far better is it to dare mighty things, to win glorious triumphs,
even though checked by failure ... than to rank with those poor
spirits who neither enjoy much nor suffer much, because they live
in a grey twilight that knows not victory nor defeat.
— Theodore Roosevelt

In The Six of Wands, our actions change from destructive to
progressive. The soul found the appropriate tools and mastered
passion into inspirational solidarity. Method appeared from
madness and order appeared from chaos. The alpha male sprung
up from the surrounding defeat and respect was born. The soul
learnt to harness his passionate nature, leading to inner and
outer respect. The picture on the card shows the alpha male
riding high on the horse of victory, with his comrades all moving
forward in the same direction as him. The Six of Wands does not
show us what we are riding into, which is a good reminder of the
polarity. Will it be battle or procession? With The Wands, it is
likely to change from one to the other incredibly quickly!

The Seven of Wands — Challenge

Only as a warrior can one withstand the path of knowledge. A warrior cannot complain or regret anything. His life is an endless challenge, and challenges cannot possibly be good or bad. Challenges are simply challenges.
— Carlos Castaneda

Sevens in the Tarot are always a test of faith (think back to The Chariot, The Seven of Swords and The Seven of Cups). The Seven of Wands questions your inner faith and makes your actions quake. The Wands, so brave, courageous, fearless, already has a number of victories under its belt. Pride maybe an issue, not knowing when to back down, just blazing forward. Back to the thin line of bravery or stupidity and it may be here that even The Wands wonder whether it has crossed that very thin line. The alpha male has swallowed his pride and come down off his high horse to defend his position. What is interesting is that if the soul could stop blazing for just one second it would recognize that they are out of harm's way, safe on higher ground as pictured in the Rider-Waite. No threat is posed by the outside, only the inner.

Hotheaded reaction and over defensiveness may create the very thing they fear, out of nothing. That is the power of creation and The Wand.

Keep battling against nothing and sooner or later you will be the cause of your own defeat. Again, we see the power of the imagination. Remember to use it wisely, so it doesn't use you. It is our creative source. Whatever we give energy to will manifest. Whatever we believe comes true. All exists as we choose to see it. We do create our reality. Of course, the reality may also be that there is a call for belief in your actions. Feeling the fear and doing it anyway. Stepping up to the mark. Convincing others by convincing yourself. Remember all cards are neutral. There is always a need to listen to your intuition and take note of the surrounding cards in the spread.

The weakness of The Wand is being so caught up in action it can't stop to think. Carried away by the past build up of fire, the quiet discernment present in the earlier stages of the two and three have burnt out of existence through to raging passion. The Wands are blessed with so much power it becomes a curse. Like King Midas. Every action creates a mess. They have to create, even if it destroys. If The Wands could stop for a second they would see there is no one there to fight. It would conserve so much energy if The Wand was put down and the soul walked away. But how can it if it is a Wand?

The Eight of Wands — High Flying

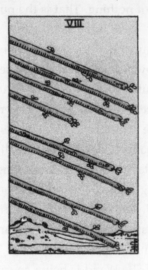

*Here the free spirit of mankind, at length, Throws its last fetters off;
and who shall place
A limit to the giant's unchained strength, Or curb his swiftness in
the forward race?*
— William Cullen Bryant

The Eight of Wands is one of the strongest, fastest cards in the
Tarot. And perhaps the strongest, fastest card of the Minor
Arcana. Eight is representative of Strength (symbol of infinity).
Strength is naturally assigned the fire sign of Leo (the strongest
of the fire signs as ruled by our strongest planet the Sun). The
Wands element is fire (the Sun). So here we have The Wands at
their height.

If we look at the picture on the card, we see The Wands
literally up in the air, streamlined. The archer's arrows of
Sagittarian vision. A picture of the strength of intent/imagination.
Imagination being used constructively. This is The Wands being
used at their best. Strength of vision, harnessed for the highest
good of all. No longer hierarchy or power imbalance, instead

through the collective exists strength in numbers.

The Eight of Wands is the perfect picture of the space, freedom and support providing the correct condition for fast powerful movement and progression to the target of your desire (The Wands). Travel, movement, friendship and inspiration are all housed here. Along with swift communications. The arrows of love and instant happenings...

The Nine of Wands — Conditioning

More than anything else, I believe it's our decisions, not the conditions of our lives, that determine our destiny.
— Anthony Robbins

The soul is one step away from its completion of its actions in The Nine of Wands. Nevertheless, the soul has expended a lot of energy in The Wands. The soul must master taming the flames and mature into the gentle inner fire of self-awareness. If it is always blazing outside of itself, it will one day burn out, just like our Sun itself.

You can see he has fought for all his Wands and been

successful. But the energetic price has been high. Feeling weakened within, the stance of protection tries to overcompensate in The Nine of Wands, now highly defensive and on guard. Unbearable, is the thought of losing at the last hurdle, expecting to have to fight to gain anything. Even the conflict in his thoughts, expend his energy. The soul has become a slave of his own nature and must learn to tame it if it is to be truly successful...

The Ten of Wands — Success?

The secret of success if learning how to use pain and pleasure instead of having pain and pleasure use you. If you do that, you're in control of your life. If you don't life controls you.
— Anthony Robbins

So the soul fought its last battle in the nine and it managed to do it, of course. Now the picture shows the struggle of the soul as it is full to its capacity. The arms crammed with all it can hold. No longer can it see the way, their vision blocked by their past actions. The energy is no longer free flowing and expressive. It is blocked. The soul is not balanced or aligned, nor is it free. It struggles to move, rather than flies high. The Wands are successful (in what we may term as success these days) so perhaps you expected a happier outcome than this hump-backed figure is denoting? Well remember each element contains the mixed blessings and lessons we need in order to evolve in the school of life.

The figure in The Ten of Wands has his success all right, but at what price? If only The Wands could put down their actions, leave their work in the office and rest assured. Then that would be real success. You can measure true success by the amount of freedom one has in their life.

The Ten of Wands stands for all those souls, not happy in their work/actions/creations but unable to drop it because of the success they have built around it. The Ten of Wands pictures perfectly the heavy price of success, and the burden of high achievement. Responsibility can become so heavy the soul can no longer have the ability to respond. How can it reach out in response without dropping all it is carrying?

Positivity/negativity/neutrality of the Wands

The Wands are warm, friendly, positive, magical, inspirational, charismatic, creative, clairvoyant, and successful, making them very attractive. Everything revolves around fire; all is drawn to the beauty of its glow and the warmth it exudes. We huddle round a hearth to warm our numb bits on a winter's day and begin feeling again. No matter the gloominess of life, when the Sun is out, everyone is, all cares melt in the heat. Our soul sings in the life — giving rays felt through the skin. Yet that very thing can also destroy. Everything revolves around the power of fire. The planets revolve around the Sun and the moth can't help but be its own demise by flying repeatedly into the flame.

Being a Leo I am definitely a Wand. Creativity pours out of

me impulsively. The older I get the more it springs forth. More and more I think oh my gosh, not again! I seem to spread myself further and wider. So much so, I am always on burn out. But paradoxically always erupting with passionate new creations. I risk creating nothing as my creativity hardly consolidates but rages on with huge amounts of passion for where I find myself at that time. Looking back at the flames behind, dulling in comparison to wherever my source is now. I know I have to go back over it if I am going to keep the flames alive. Yet the moving forward never stops either. My distance travelled continues to be far and wide (seven hundred miles a week to be exact!) It sure is knackering all right! So many times my impulsive actions bulk at being restricted, and on many occasions, I have definitely been my own worst enemy. Like the time spirit told me the lottery numbers and I told them I was in too much of a rush to listen so I would compromise with them! Going to the till, I felt every cell in my body screaming to me to stop and wait. But still my arrogant, ever moving nature burnt forward, burning right through a win of 4.5 million, leaving me with two tenners (the result of three numbers on each line!). Now that is the power of The Seven of Wands for you! I like to think I am living and learning, cultivating that gentle flame of inner awareness!

Working with The Wands
Write about a chapter in your life that felt like The Wands, and assign each step one of the wand cards. What did you learn? (Or, have you learnt from looking at it this way?)

Is there an area in your life now that feels like The Wands? It could be in your work, your home, your friendships, relationships, or your mind, heart or body. Where are you at with it? Give it a Wand card. Where were you at with it a month ago? Two months ago? Three months ago? Are you going backwards and forwards? Keep a monthly diary. A month from today come back and see, have you moved forwards or backwards? Keep in mind that sometimes we have to go backwards to go forwards. Remember not to fall into the blame game (of yourself or others)...

Chapter 13

The Pentacles — The Law of Manifestation

After the thought (Swords) induced feelings (Cups) and sparked action (Wands), we are left with the manifestation of all that went before in The Pentacles, the end result. The Pentacle is what we have to show for our blood, sweat and tears. It is our just deserts. Whatever we sow, we reap. The element that represents Pentacles is earth. Earth is the realm of things we can see and touch. Matter is the densest vibration there is so The Pentacles house some of the slowest and heaviest cards in the Tarot, as well as the most reliable and secure. In The Pentacles, the soul is left with the result of his actions. Like Gandhi said, "Thoughts create feeling, feeling creates action, action creates manifestation, so let's make sure our thoughts are good".

The Ace of Pentacles — Manifestation

Every great work, every great accomplishment, has been brought into manifestation through holding to the vision, and often just before the big achievement comes apparent failure and discouragement.

— Florence Scovel Shinn

All aces picture beginnings, so in The Pentacles we have the beginning of manifestation. The soul has gone through the stages of thought (Swords), feeling (Cups) and action (Wands). Now left with its beautifully carved out creation (Pentacle). The Pentacle is birth of the tangible. Perhaps an actual baby, or a creative one resulting in a new business, career, home or other tangible beginning. The Ace of Pentacles represents the beginning of end result. The baby has just been born, the ribbons cut, the contracts signed, the keys are now exchanged, unless there are other signs showing that the manifestation maybe struggling to appear in some way.

The Two of Pentacles — Juggling

Communication is a continual balancing act, juggling the conflicting needs for intimacy and independence. To survive in the world, we have to act in concert with others, but to survive as ourselves, rather than simply cogs in a wheel, we have to act alone.
— Deborah Tannen

As always the ace grew into two. In The Two of Pentacles, we have the juggling of two earthly manifestations. Maybe the baby born is a twin, or second child. Maybe you are having to juggle your time with work and home. Maybe the new home has been found but there is a chain. Perhaps you just started up your business but can't leave your old career yet. Perhaps two jobs have been taken on because income is equalling expenditure, (or just for variety). Here we see the student juggling work with studies and the working mum juggling her family and career demands. The possible manifestations of The Two of Pentacles are limitless. But the energy behind them is always the same.

It is a time of great expense in the soul's energy. Just like the juggler, he mustn't take his eye of a thing for a moment if he is to keep it all going. The Two of Pentacles can feel torturous in that it seems there is no end in sight. Zigzagging along rather than aiming straight for the target. The soul feels caught up in the demands of daily routine and unable to see the way out. An unending cycle, as pictured by the symbol of infinity acting like handcuffs. But sooner or later something has to change, it always does...

Three of Pentacles — Growth

Remember, if you ever need a helping hand, it's at the end of your arm, as you get older, remember you have another hand: The first is to help yourself, the other is help others.
— Audrey Hepburn

In The Three of Pentacles, the soul has progressed from the treadmill into expansion. A third influence has come along to make the change happen, perhaps an investor, a helping hand from friends or family, an employee, a new opportunity or set of skills. Again, the manifestations of The Three of Pentacles are limitless. But the energy behind is the same, expansion. As we are looking at solid things we can touch in the realm of the Pentacle, this would apply to things that provide us with structure and security. We looked at the career side above, but this would also apply to home. Perhaps an extension or improvement (as the picture seems to suggest) or a further property being acquired for business. As always, you would need to listen to the information in the spread and your intuition for the answer. Now do you see why the last reader your saw sighed when you asked them "what does that card mean?" If so, wait until we get to the court cards!

The Four of Pentacles — Security?

Those who desire to give up freedom in order to gain security will not have, nor do they deserve, either one.
— Benjamin Franklin

With fours, we reach stability. Structure and security, don't we all long for that? Perhaps more so in the realm of Pentacles than anywhere else. Oh! To know that we will have enough for all our tomorrows!

Because Pentacles represent the fourth element of earth, it's like we have a double four in The Four of Pentacles. If you double four you get eight (Strength). Whenever there is strength there is or has been the experience of challenge.

The soul has gone through so much to get its first foot-holding that it is desperate to stay there. This is where we get to the challenge of the four. The soul becomes strong in its wrongness. If we hang on too much we confine ourselves. We become frozen with fear. This happened to me once, hanging off a cliff face. Crying with fear, unable to breathe, hyperventilating with panic. I had my foothold, but I felt if I moved a muscle I wouldn't. (Luckily I skipped the fall of The Five of Pentacles and went straight into the Six of Aid!) How can we lift that hand to let go of where we are now if we feel it will be our downfall? Yet we also know we can't continue living the way we are. The flow of life force will eventually dry up. No movement, no life.

The person pictured in the card has a Pentacle over his crown chakra showing how his attachment has disconnected him to spirit and caused a heavy head. He clasps it close to his chest blocking his heart and consequently his ability to live or breathe. We also find a Pentacle under each foot. His whole path has become about the material world and this has cut his connection to the real earth, the earth that matters. Subsequently he has become ungrounded and insecure. The opposite of what this card is supposed to mean. Supposed is the operative word as remember all cards are neutral.

In the fours, we have security, but security can be stifling and no more so than in the realm of the Pentacle. The danger is being so tight that you strangle the life out of the flow (a danger we also saw in the fourth trump of The Emperor). How can you move forward when you are so weighed down? How can you reach out to attain more when your arms are so full of what you are holding onto?

I often see The Four of Pentacles when a client is feeling

insecure. When probed they will talk to me of financial or practical concerns. But The Four of Pentacles also talks about how security can paradoxically make you more insecure. If insecurity is there I would bet your bottom dollar (excuse the pun) it is an inner thought/feeling/action that is creating it. Change that and all will change. The saying "what you never had, you will never miss" is very true of human nature.

Once we ascertain a certain level that we have worked so hard for and desired for so long the attachment becomes a prison of confinement. The fear of losing what we had can be more torturous than not having in the first place.

The Five of Pentacles— Poverty

Contentment is natural wealth, luxury is artificial poverty.
— Socrates

In all fives, we have the beginning of change, which usually presents chaos as the old structure is dismantled. In The Five of Pentacles, the lesson of the four is being truly learnt. The soul ended up manifesting its own fear. It didn't change its thoughts.

It just carried on trying to attain more — and we looked at why that was impossible. Perhaps the soul was on a journey of self-sabotage because it couldn't take the pressure. My first boyfriend ran away from home at fifteen and survived in different circuses, squats and streets until at twenty-four the council finally gave him a flat. He couldn't cope with it. He didn't know how to say no to all his homeless peers that used it as a doss hole. He didn't know how to pay the bills that were mounting up because of it. Even simple things like setting up a direct debit seemed an impossible mountain to climb because he didn't have the equipment or training. Even though he knew it was a stage of change that could lead to a better life in the long run, he couldn't cope. One day he got up and walked out, back to a life on the streets, leaving his peers with his roof over their heads. When we have been one way for so long, when something is deeply ingrained how can we cope with that change?

The Tarot teaches us that what we think, we create. That is never as apparent as in the manifestations of The Pentacles. The fives are notorious for containing hard lessons. So, here is the hard lesson of being our own downfall, our own worst enemy. Through fear, the soul created loss. In Pentacles, we see physical loss, in solid matter, land, money, or body. The Five of Pentacles could be expressed as loss of health, income, home, business etc. The soul has fallen upon hard times (albeit of their own doing). Remembering that all cards are neutral/dual, there is as always a reason:

The Five of Pentacles rips The Pentacle from the soul's crown, once again invoking the connection to spirit (even if only through seeking solace). The pentacle is prized from the heart, causing the soul to feel and breathe again. Have you ever noticed that during hard times certain bonds strengthen? And finally, The Pentacles are taken from the feet, reconnecting the soul with a sense of deep rooted balance. Reminding them of the funda-mentals of life and restoring calm. The soul is now well connected once again, from the crown to the feet and balanced in the heart centre.

As I write this, I think about the time I got an iPod. I listened to it so much that every now and again I would hear spirit shouting "you aren't listening to us anymore"; I promised I would listen less. But I didn't. I got some new earphones instead and they were so good I listened even more! The first warning came when I lost them.

All panicked because of my attachment I was relieved when spirit told me they were on the passenger seat of the car. Once again, they warned me I wasn't listening enough and once again I told them I would listen to it less. I didn't! Soon after that, I lost my iPod! But far from being distressed, I was actually relieved. I felt this freedom and delight sweep through me with overwhelming joy of being reconnected with spirit. In fact, I was so happy and grateful that a month later I got a phone call from someone who found it!

On a more serious note, The Work of Byron Katie comes to mind. Byron Katie is a famous therapist who asks a set of four questions to detach a person from their story. She works with souls in The Five of Pentacles all the time. They are attached to their story, their "poor me" poverty consciousness. In The Five of Pentacles, there still is a challenge of attachment, even though fives enforce change. With Pentacles we are at the most solid, one-track level of energy. In The Five of Pentacles, the soul can reach a certain level of spirituality but get stuck there. Just take a look at the fixed earth sign Taurus, notorious for its dislike of change, resisting it with all its might, even if it would be a change for the better. The soul becomes attached to the experience of The Five of Pentacles, it becomes the story of their life and the ego identifies with it. But then again there is always the other side of the story.

The Six of Pentacles — Charity

Charity is no substitute for justice withheld.
— Saint Augustine

As in all sixes, we have reached a stage of progression. In The Six of Pentacles we see aid, the helping hand, not unlike The Three of Pentacles (but twice as strong in the six). But in the picture we see the soul on its knees, with charity being given. Charity comes in many forms, the state, employment, family and friends, the NHS, NGOs NFPs, as always the possible manifestations go on. Although this looks like improvement, there is the other side of the coin. The stances are no longer even, as if they were in The Three of Pentacles. The status quo is out of balance. Balance and fairness is a key issue here as signified by the scales pictured in the card. The soul has become indebted.

Take the homeless drug addict who is given a house, in the same area of where all their addicted friends are because they have to stay at the same methadone clinic. They can never leave because of the script and because they are on jobseekers. Every time a peer falls off the wagon, they pull them off too. The environment that seems to be aiding you with one hand, keeps you there with the other. The saying "selling your soul to the devil" or "the poor get poorer and the rich get richer" fit nicely here. Even helping hands from friends and family can come with conditions or hidden expectations. Without rescue, there is no hope and there is also no politics.

The Seven of Pentacles — Determination

A man can be as great as he wants to be. If you believe in yourself and have the courage, the determination, the dedication, the competitive drive and if you are willing to sacrifice the little things in life and pay the price for the things that are worthwhile, it can be done.
— Vince Lombardi

The message in the seven is one of endurance. In The Seven of Pentacles, we see the toughest manifestation of determination, conviction and resolve. The soul has learnt about its self sabotaging thoughts, it has realized that if it is to ever escape the stalemate of the six it has to feed, water and nurture itself with the right thoughts.

The soul has done this patiently and is starting to recoup independence. Diligently nurturing, caring and watching over the nest egg. Still, just like in The Two of Pentacles the expense of energy far out ways the return in the short term.

Nevertheless, the soul has learnt all the lessons that went before including those in the two. It now has a more matter of fact attitude creating the well-earthed blessings of calmness and patience. If the surrounding cards or message is different to what is said above this card shows a pointer of the best attitude to adopt.

The Eight of Pentacles — Achievement

Without continual growth and progress, such words as improvement, achievement, and success have no meaning.
— Benjamin Franklin

The soul has been through so much! It created it all, and lost it all. In The Eight, we always see strength so in The Eight of Pentacles we see strength of manifestations. The patience and endurance in the seven is now paying dividends. Here we see the strength of skill, the skill of manifestation. Now the soul just continues to build strength upon strength as pictured by The Pentacles stacking up, looking like the proverbial career ladder. Our investments boom, whether it is in property, business or just the pure skill of survival. Our D.I.Y disasters turn into our D.I.Y dreams.

The Nine of Pentacles— Self Sufficiency

Happiness belongs to the self-sufficient.
— Aristotle

The soul has reached the heights of its own manifestations. The Nine of Pentacles is similar to The Nine of Cups where it seems the journey has reached a destination, but with all nines, there is still a step to go. However, as self-satisfaction goes this is the cream of the crop! This is the life. The one the soul dreamed of, the one it worked for, the one it lost, the one it regained, with even more strength. The life of ease and comfort. They say you can tell how wealthy a person is, not by the size of their bank account but by the choice in their life. Now they also say that money can't buy you happiness, but it can buy you choices! Although this is true on one level, if there is even a little bit of attachment left to the four or five then what appears wealthy is not.

Take the soul that moves into their mother's house to support her and pay the mortgage after the death of their father. Even though it's the last place they want to be. Until they can un-attach from the feeling of duty no amount of money will buy their freedom. Yet on the other hand, this card does picture that place of total self-sufficiency. The soul has released itself from selling itself to the Devil. Here we have the car, the house, the garden, the lifestyle. And as I said before as long as we have totally dis-attached from the process of the four and five then we have true independence and abundant choice and it feels good! Deeper than that, the inner manifestations that are harder to see, but able to feel. They tell us that we have achieved true self worth. The outside manifestations are but a mere mirror.

Ten of Pentacles— The Money Tree

The finest gift you can give anyone is encouragement. Yet, almost no one gets the encouragement they need to grow to their full potential. If everyone received the encouragement they need to grow, the genius in most everyone would blossom and the world would produce abundance beyond the wildest dreams. We would have more than one Einstein, Edison, Schweitzer, Mother Theresa, Dr. Salk and other great minds in a century.
— Sidney Madwed

Tens show the end of one cycle and the beginning of another, which is why in The Ten of Pentacles I have decided to use the analogy of the money tree. We take cuttings from trees, plant them in the soil and they multiply, of course, over time, with slow patient dedication as they are new aces. Nevertheless apply what we learnt and one day we will have an orchard.

In The Ten of Pentacles, not only has the soul reached its destination but it is aware that achievement with no ongoing purpose is an empty experience. There is a need to put the success to good use. Help the younger generations in family or society.

The Ten of Pentacles is a card of tradition and values, of chains, corporates and capitalism, of the rich getting richer and money breeding money, the Freemasons and the Paris Hilton of this world. Do you feel any repulsion at that comment? If so maybe you are still hung up on the four and the five? True abundance comes when we can wish it for everyone.

A very powerful abundance meditation is one where we visualize our worst enemy being abundant and practice wishing that for them.

Of course, it could simply mean that all your hard work has paid off, that you have reached a point where you can support yourself, and your family. Maybe even to the point where the responsibility has turned into an investment that takes care of you. If you can't see it yet, maybe it's about the nature to adopt.

Positivity/negativity/neutrality of The Pentacles

The Pentacles are slow, steady and solid. They are the basis of everything. The stuff of necessity. The very thing we can rely and depend upon — earth.

We may think that we crave to be in a comfortable place, albeit home, career or relationship. So why when we have it do we yearn for more? More money, a bigger home, a better relationship maybe. What we yearn for really is the feeling of living that comes from The Swords through to The Wands. Pentacles represent a destination point. We are living, growing, changing, evolving, journeying. Arriving leaves us with a niggling feeling that there must be more. A desire to journey on arises. Of course, we can still grow with The Pentacles. In fact, they deliver the promise of growth more than any other element. We need earth to plant. But if you are feeling urgency in your veins are you going to be able to sit there and wait for the tree to grow? Particularly with The Swords filling your head with inspired ideas, The Cups drifting you into daydreams and The

Wands tempting you excitement, drama and life?

After three years of struggle to keep the doors open to my first holistic centre, finances began to show promise of growth. Yet I made the decision to close. Others thought I was nuts! All this work for three years just to close? "That's it — I always thought she was a bit strange but she's proper crazy!"

What they didn't understand was that I had arrived. I had grown and I could not grow anymore. In order to do that I had to move on. The Swords swashbuckled around my head with new visions. The promise of freedom filled my head. The Cups cracked open my heart so that I could no longer deny the forthcoming flow of dreams, igniting The Wands branding creativity into my veins. I couldn't express it in my little confine of four walls. I had taken the trip and grown too big. I could have waited another year or so and then got someone in as a manager, but the feeling of heaviness and responsibility that went with that was a weight around me pulling me down. The dream come true had become my prison. We may dream of achievement, but it's about the journey more than we realise.

Working with The Pentacles
Write about a chapter in your life that felt like The Pentacles, and assign each step one of the Pentacle cards. What did you learn? (Or have you learnt from looking at it this way?)

Is there an area in your life now that feels like The Pentacles? It could be in your work, your home, your friendships, relationships, or your mind, heart or body. Where are you at with it? Give it a Pentacle card. Where were you at with it a month ago? Two months ago? Three months ago? Are you going backwards and forwards? Keep a monthly diary. A month from today come back and see, have you moved forwards or backwards? Keep in mind that sometimes we have to go backwards to go forwards. Remember not to fall into the blame game (of yourself or others)...

Chapter 14

The Court Cards Demystified — Meet The Tarot Family

So here we have arrived at the notorious court cards, known as every readers nightmare! Oh how many questions do I get about how do you read court cards? And complaints that Tarot books gloss over them. Here I endeavour to make tangible the intangible.

Court cards are archetypal. Just like the Major Arcana. The expression of court cards can be difficult to pin down, just like the Major Arcana. And this is why the Minor Arcana is not so minor. The Minor Arcana pastes the labels and sticks them on. A spread with just Major or court cards can be almost impossible to read unless you have a very well trained intuition. As court cards are archetypal their primary representation is a just a type of energy. Energy expresses itself in many different ways. Be thankful that in the case of the court cards it's narrowed down to one of three ways. These are:

- An expression of an inner personality within the client that is trying to come through
- A person in the client's life
- A situation or message (depending on the card, we look at this further on).

Reading court cards is not as straightforward as the famous line of "there's a tall, dark handsome stranger" or "there's a man here with pale skin, blue eyes and fair hair, sensitive, dreamy, and introverted, over forty" (stereotypical King of Cups) or "there is a dark haired, stocky young man about to leave university and become an accountant" (typical Knight of Pentacles). If it was it would mean all businessmen/women would be stocky with dark hair and all sensitive people would possess blonde hair and blue eyes!

We humans are complex. We possess multifaceted personas. Look at all the different expressions of who you are. Who are you at home, at work, with family and different friends?

There may be a common denominator, but the expression of energy changes with whatever it comes into contact with.

Take Jim. At the bank Jim is seen as a confident laugh a second, but when at home with mum he becomes James who feels like he just did something wrong. Jack the lad with his girl colleagues, they giggle and fantasise about what an exciting boyfriend he'd be. But behind closed doors he becomes Mr boring in the company of his serious girlfriend Joan. In fact he even calls her "Joan the moan" when he is down the pub with fellow football friends. When James sees his friend sensitive, spiritual Steve, something stirs. What once felt funny now feels remorseful. Steve triggered the emotional part in James and cracked something open that no one else could.

Do you ever find yourself discussing a mutual friend to someone and they say, "What Steve? Did that? No way!". As you compare your notes you see more and more differences, to the point you wonder if you are talking about the same person.

This demonstrates that even if you have identified The Knight of Cups as a person in the client's life rather than part of the client, it is still an expression of energy being released in that person's life and therefore in them. Taking this further, it shows not only a part of them, but also a message!

Remember everything/everyone in our lives is just a mirror with a message for us. Therefore, it may be more accurate to describe court cards as a person in someone's life that is bringing out a new side to them and showing them something. So that means court cards can mean all three interpretations at once! But there are times that you will need to pin it down to one for the sake of clarity. As I said before, things just aren't that straightforward with the court cards.

Court cards seem like they are there to test our ability to use our intuition and story tell.

Nevertheless, I shall as I said before try to make tangible the intangible. In doing so, I will be putting the court cards in boxes. But you would do well to remember they are living breathing expressions of energy that like you to step out of the box with them.

To clarify, the court cards represent a part of ourselves, a person, a message, opportunity or an event (depending on which court card) or all of the above.

Below you will all the information you need relating to each court card, but the best practice is to read it and forget it. Trust your subconscious absorbed it like a sponge and will all knowingly intuitively pop up with the right answer. The moment you start thinking "is it this or that?" you will be coming out of your intuitive right brain and accessing your analytical left brain, which is famous for blocking readings.

Kings — Expressed as a person (or part of self) they represent men, or women expressing a masculine energy. Over forty or possessing that level of maturity. As a message, they represent business or the ability to become accomplished within the field suggested by their suit.

Queens — Expressed as a person (or part of self) they represent women, or men expressing a feminine energy. Over the age of forty or possessing that level of maturity. As a message, they represent society and an ability to be responsive in whatever field is suggested by their suit.

Knights — Expressed as a person we see a young or emotionally immature man, woman (or part of self) with characteristics belonging to the particular suit. As a message Knights bring opportunities, what type depends on the suit.

Pages — Expressed as a person we see an actual child, inner child or a vulnerable part of ourselves with characteristics belonging to the particular suit. Pages are messengers, bringing news related to their suits. The news is likely to be of fresh or new young things. In this way, it may be helpful to see the Pages as Aces.

The Astrological Key of The Court Cards

As said previously we are multifaceted beings. However there is usually an underlying essence of a person, which we will call the base note. The base note provides the foundation of the being from which other personas appear and disappear, but the base note remains there. The base note is easily determined by Astrology. Therefore, some knowledge of Astrology is useful for the study of Tarot and vice versa. Understanding of the Tarot is enriched by Astrological knowledge, and greatly eases interpretation of the (court) cards.

The Swords Family — As discussed in the chapter on The Swords they represent the element of air. Air houses thought and spirit. The psyche (which means both mind and spirit). Hard formality and flexible adaptability. The strike of genius, communication and movement. The air signs are Gemini, Libra, Aquarius. In appearance, they are known to be tall, hard, thin and wiry — just like The Swords. But don't let that type casting keep you in a box.

The Cup Family — As discussed in the chapter on The Cups they represent the element of water. Water houses emotion and feeling, the heart and gut felt intuition. Heartfelt expression and dreamy creativity. Sentimentality and sensitivity, femininity and passivity. The water signs are Cancer, Scorpio and Pisces. In appearance, they are likely to be flowing, quiet, curvy, pale and pillowy. But don't let that limit you.

The Wand Family — As discussed in the chapter on The Wands they represent the element of fire. Fire houses creation, passion and action. Drama, excitement, fun, obsession and destruction. Here we move from the introverted to the extroverted, from the passive to the active, from the feminine to the masculine. The fire signs are Aries, Leo and Sagittarius. In appearance, they are likely to be fiery, charismatic and loud, but don't be bound by it.

The Pentacle Family — As discussed in the chapter on The Pentacles they represent the element of earth. Earth houses achievement and stability. The body and physical world such as structure and career. Practical organisation and business acumen. The earth signs are Virgo, Capricorn and Taurus. In appearance, they are likely to be short, stocky and dark. But as I said previously, don't be bound by appearances.

At the beginning of this chapter, we discussed how we are multi-faceted beings. We are made not just of our Sun signs. Where all the planets were at the time of our birth will affect our being. Particularly what sign the Moon occupies (which determines our emotional nature) and what planet was rising over the horizon. Known as the rising sign it governs our appearance (which is why I was saying not to get too bound by the appearances). For instance I am a Leo with Taurus rising and appear a mix of Wands and Pentacles. I have red hair, but it has become darker as I got older and borders on brown. I differ from the normal Wand in that instead of pale skin and blue eyes I have brown eyes and darker skin. (Taurus Ascendant). I do still have freckles; they appear only when the Sun is out. Because Taurus and Leo are both fixed my appearance is more short and stocky rather than the fast, athletic appearance of The Wand.

My granddad was well known in the village I grew up in as he had a shop there and five short daughters (with rather ample behinds). When I was seventeen, I was in the local, which housed an Irish landlord. A punter said, "You're not Mr Read's grand-daughter are you?"

The landlord replied for me, "A cors she is cant you tell she gat er ass near da grund!" (A typical Leo/Taurus trait!).

I have The Wand personality — active, creative, extroverted and charismatic (not to mention full of myself!). But my Taurus ascendant also grounds that activity into manifestation, determi-nation and commitment (which grounds the ego and produces one tracked habits!). Both Leo and Taurus are fixed, dependable, loyal and head strong, so I have a double helping of those qualities.

My husband is not only Gemini, but has five planets in Gemini. This would make him like a bunch of helium balloons going high in the sky, but when people meet him they think he is a Taurus (which was my first impression too). He possesses such a strong laid-back groundedness you would never believe he has five planets in Gemini (until you get to know him better!). This is because both his ascendant and Moon are in Taurus and as the Moon is exalted (at its happiest) in Taurus, he has a very strong energy of Taurus. Thank God for that, or he really would be off the planet. You can see the mix of Gemini with Taurus in his appearance, tall, wiry and going grey early like a Sword. Being half-Italian he is also dark like The Pentacle.

What I am trying to show you is that it is always better to describe the energy of what a Court Card represents rather than assign it a particular sign; for instance if a reader said to me, "is your husband a Taurus?". My answer would be "no". Yet if they said, "your partner seems to possess Taurean type qualities of dependability, loyalty and earthy groundedness", I would say "yes".

Below are some keywords for each of the energies associated with the Court families. But remember people are a mix:

Personas

Air Signs (The Sword Family)
The characteristics of Swords are speedy thoughts or neurotic analysis, interest in the psyche, values intellect and communication. Changeable, free and unpredictable. Confused and ungrounded, or the other extreme, convinced of their opinions. Fighting for fairness and justice (or their interpretation of it). Academic genius, eccentric erratic and unnerving. Quirky, talkative and sharp. Knowledge, strength of mind, speech, and head ruling the heart.

Water Signs (The Cup Family)
Fluidly deep. Introverted, intuitive and mysterious. Unbounded, passive and confused. Easily influenced. Empathic psychic sponge. Caring and nurturing, containing issues of conditional and unconditional love. Vulnerable, protective, defensive, and manipulative. Dreamy and mystical. Sensitive, artistic, musical, creative and emotional. Heart ruling the head.

Fire Signs (The Wand Family)
Dynamic, active, creative and full on. Motivated, busy, intense and energetic. Warm, friendly and expressive. Overbearing, obsessive, dominating and controlling. Attention seeking and extroverted. Fast, expressive, impulsive, passionate and charismatic. Infectious, inspirational and impulsive. Young and fun. Dramatic. Hotheaded.

Earth Signs (The Pentacle Family)
Thorough, dedicated, committed and focussed. Determined, patient, reliable and loyal. Organised, practical, realistic and

down to earth. Sensual, slow, steady, deep and calm. Nurturing, protective, supportive and responsible. Retentive, anal, stubborn, materialistic and business-minded.

Events

As events, here is the key for each Court Card:

The Sword Family

- *Page of Swords* — communication, letters, emails, phone calls.
- *Knight of Swords* — opportunity to express your opinions.
- *Queen of Swords* — communication opportunity with community.
- *King Of Swords* — important communications and decisions in business.

The Cup Family

- *Page of Cups* — message of feelings.
- *Knight of Cups* — heartfelt opportunity.
- *Queen of Cups* — caring for community.
- *King of Cups* — intuition and gut feelings in business.

The Wand Family

- *Page of Wands* — message of action.
- *Knight of Wands* — motivation, get up and go, opportunity for movement.
- *Queen of Wands* — action in community.
- *King of Wands* — action in business.

The Pentacle Family

- *Page of Pentacles* — message of achievement.
- *Knight of Pentacles* — opportunity to set goals.
- *Queen of Pentacles* — commitment to a cause.

- *King of Pentacle* — achievement in business.

Determination of Expression

In order to determine whether the court card represents a persona of the client, someone in the client's life or an event, look at where the card has landed. Spreads can be very handy with court cards, for instance if a court card turns up in the position of the self in the spread it answers the question for you. Just like if it turned up in the position of "best course of action". Trickier is if a court card falls in the place of "unexpected influences". In that case, it could show a person or an event. Trickier still is when you free flow or story-tell. In the latter two cases, you will need to ask yourself the following:

- What is the flavour and general message of the spread?
- What does my intuition tell me?

Meet The Sword Family

Mr Sword (King) — In academic employment of the mind (lawyer, doctor, psychologist, MP) Likely to have his head stuck in a book, newspaper or gadget. Not comfortable with emotion. Values intellectual development of his children. Education, morals and values. Shows his wife he loves her through ways other than outpouring of emotions.

Mrs Sword (Queen) — Previously divorced, widowed or suffered other loss. Hardened to emotion. Can be bitter and cynical. Incredibly strong and loyal friend, incredibly strong and sharp enemy. Quick to judge, analytical. Razor sharp vision sees right through, doesn't suffer fools gladly. Hates any kind of unfairness or injustice. Sharp. Maybe a lawyer, doctor, scientist or headteacher in a private school. Values intellectual development. Un-maternal.

Stella Sword (Knight) — University student, political activist, possesses courage of her convictions, believes the pen is mightier than the sword, surprising, unpredictable, hard to keep up with, strong willed, rushes in where angels fear to tread.

Socrates Sword (Page) — inquisitive, into everything. Showing promise of a great mind, but easily confused. Short attention span, restless, talkative. Highly strung, reactive, anxious.

Bringing The Sword Family Alive

- Who in your life do you recognise as one of the Sword cards? Perhaps your Dad is a typical King of Swords? Or perhaps he is more a Queen of Swords and your mum is more like The King? What about your boss? Your best friend? The guy who owns the corner shop?

- Once you have placed them find out their star-sign. Don't worry if it's not air, as I explained before they could have a lot of air in their chart. Quite often we see the ascendant (rising sign) most as that is what a person portrays to the world.

- Who in your life brings out The King, Queen, Knight and The Page of Swords in you? Why? Perhaps there is a mix of personas? Can you see how you change when coming into contact with different energies? Write about the roles and dynamics.

Notes:

Meet The Cups Family

KING of CUPS.

Mr Cup (King) — Very comfortable with his feminine side and expression of emotions. Perhaps somewhat flamboyant, but sensitive at the same time. Likely to be a social worker or in some type of helping profession, openly affectionate. Adoring of his partner and children. Could be quirky and musical. Spiritual and dreamy. Mystical.

Mrs Cup (Queen) — Overly feminine so can be an excellent mother and wife, but can also be overly emotional. Caring can turn into smothering over protectiveness and moody manipulation. Unconditional loves becomes or masks conditional. Intuitive, creative, maybe musical or artistic in some way. Empathic, likely to be a counsellor or therapist. A lot of emphasis is put on talking about feelings.

KNIGHT of CUPS.

Cassie Cup (Knight) — Doing a degree in fine art, music, or social work. Has close friends but sensitive so has to be careful about the company she keeps. Has been easily influenced, blackmailed and manipulated in the past. Would prefer to play her violin, write poems, paint or chill with her best friend than go down the student bar.

PAGE of CUPS.

Quentin Cup (Page) — A very sensitive, introverted and quiet young chap that finds the world hard to bear. Finds other children cruel, often bullied for being "a wet sissy". Spends most of his time talking to his imaginary friend or hiding behind his mum's skirt.

Bringing The Cup Family Alive

- Who in your life do you recognise as one of The Cups? Perhaps your granddad loves to wear that embarrassing flamboyant shirt that brings out a mystical look in his eyes? Maybe your male or female boss puts an emphasis on talking things through. What friends fit these personas? What enemies perhaps?

- Once you have placed them find out their star-sign. Don't worry if it's not water. As I explained before they could have a lot of water in their chart. If they are open to getting a chart and you looking it can be interesting to see. Particularly if they have a water Moon or ascendant.

- Put yourself next to these cards. How does your base note change? Do different people bring out a different side to you enough for you to have to change cards? This is a great exercise to do as you see everyone fits into a stereotype. It can help you understand why they are the way they are. This fosters more understanding in relationships as well as deepening your relationship with the Tarot.

Notes:

Meet The Wand Family

Mr Wand (King) — Extroverted and chatty, the life and soul of the party. Adores attention and loves people. Charismatic, likes the ladies. Passionate, warm and sociable. Possesses dynamic energy and the gift of the gab. Persuasive, influential and inspirational. Sells himself for a living, from salesman to actor etc. Great dad as a big kid himself. Has a zest for life, lives for fun. Contagious! May find it hard to laugh at himself, may be more sensitive than he lets on, may have a serious male ego or pride issue. Dominating, controlling.

Mrs Wand (Queen) — Is superwoman! She works full time running her own creative business and does it all herself, from the designs to the promotions and sales. Up at the crack of dawn to the gym before work. Stops to shop on the way home, prepares a banquet for her husband's clients. The house is in ship shape condition, even though she has her elderly mother and five children under seven. Two of which she adopted from an orphanage in Romania (think famous Queen of Wands Madonna). She is also a member of every committee you can think of not in the least the Parent Teacher Association! Maybe a bit controlling! Finds it hard to let go. Loves people, loves to be sociable and on the go. But can take on too much and get stressed. She sees a lot (clairvoyantly— the light of fire helps us see), finds it hard not to react to it. Impulsive. Creative. Dynamic.

KNIGHT of WANDS.

Willie Wand (Knight) — Is off on a gap year travelling the world after trying this and that in uni. He feels too creative to be put in a box; it gets too slow and boring. He becomes disruptive, bunks off and drives round town in his boy racer with music blaring. Girls drop at his feet and he drops them like hot potatoes. He is the envy of his fellow lads who wonder how he does it (and gets away with it).

Wanda Wand — Is forever ripping her trousers at school whilst she is climbing trees with the lads and making gagging noises when they try to kiss her. When it's time to be learning she often tries proclaiming she is stuck up the tree. Always pushing boundaries. At home, she loves her noisy boys toys (if she can stay indoors, out of a tree or beating a boy up that is!) Her excessive energy may need to be channelled into something more productive, like performing arts.

Bringing The Wand Family Alive

- Who in your life do you recognise as one of The Wands? Did your uncle always get down in rough and tumble with you whilst flirting with your mum (his sister-in-law!)? Perhaps your mum is the equivalent to Mrs Bucket (Bouquet!) from keeping up experiences — oh imagine flirting with her — or Madonna (the other wand type)! Perhaps you are secretly jealous of your best friend's popularity? Similarly maybe your partner drives you insane with their ability to push the boundaries and melt you into putty.
- Once you have placed The Wand people in your life find out their star-sign. Don't worry if it's not fire. As I

explained before they could have a lot of fire in their chart. Nevertheless, it is interesting if it is immediately apparent or they are happy to let you look into their chart.

- Who in your life brings out The King, Queen, Knight and The Page of Wands in you? Why? Perhaps there is a mix of personas, but can you see how you change when coming into contact with different energies?

Notes:

Meet The Pentacles Family

KING ⚜ PENTACLES.

Mr Pentacle (King) — Reliable, dependable, predictable, family man. Also a business man. Highly professional. Maybe an accountant or advisor. Loyal, committed, steadfast. Not a fast moving character, some call him boring. All work and no play. But after the kids have their routine bedtime a very private sensual side comes forth for Mrs Pentacles eyes only!

Mrs Pentacle (Queen) — Used to be an investment banker in the city, but gave it up when they moved to the country to have kids. Now a stay at home mum, she likes nothing more than getting her wellies on and looking after the chickens, cows and allotment. She gets so much from nurturing life, in all forms. A very secure, grounded and nurturing mother with a serious air of responsibility. She gets the children involved in daily routines from the word go. She doesn't miss the city or her high flying life, like she thought she might. She feels so fulfilled by the land and children, not to mention fulfilling her husband's needs!

Percy Pentacle — Studying accountancy hard. Somewhat shy and awkward in social situations. Stubborn. He comes across as a stuck up, arrogant, patronising little know it all! But actually has a very kind heart and is just too old for his years so gets on better with adults. An animal lover, he adores his rabbit. Already looking at investments and pensions, making provisions for when his parents get old.

PAGE of PENTACLES.

Pearl Pentacle — Is top in her year at school, in everything! Praised by her family for her achievements she doesn't understand why she gets bullied for the same thing at school. Comes from such a nurturing background she doesn't understand the big wide world. Bullied for being a geeky teacher's pet through school, she turns in on herself. Pearl doesn't have a lot of friends. But she loves the animals she helps mum look after and already knows she wants to be a vet when she grows up— that doesn't ever change.

- Who in your life do you recognise as one of The Pentacles? Perhaps your annoying older brother who gets good grades in everything and is always praised by your parents. Maybe your mum is a real earth mother? What friends fit these personas? What enemies perhaps?
- Once you have placed them find out their star-sign. Don't worry if it's not an earth sign. As I explained before they could have a lot of earth in their chart. It's just interesting to see, particularly if they are happy to explore the rest of their chart, and particularly if they have an earth Moon or ascendant.

- Who in your life brings out The King, Queen, Knight and The Page of Pentacles in you? Why? Perhaps there is a mix of personas? Can you see how you change when coming into contact with different energies? Write them down.

Notes:

So Which One Is Your Base Note?

Come back to yourself:

- List all your talents, qualities, gifts, strengths, challenges and weaknesses. Are you logical? Sensitive? Creative? Or down to earth? Do you love to be out and about (Wands) or at home (Cups/Pentacles)? Are you a pleasure seeker (Wands) or an achiever (Pentacles)? A creative (Wands) or academic (Swords/Pentacles)? Are you primarily a visual (Wands) or feeling person (Cups)?

As you see, some qualities belong to more than one suit. You are likely to find yourself a mix but still one, perhaps two will be the strongest and this will be your base note. You can take this further by getting your birth chart done and seeing how strong each element is that you are made up from. Taking into particular consideration the personal planets of the Moon and Ascendant/rising sign.

Going back to my chart as an example, I really identify with The Queen Of Wands (Leo Sun) and The Queen of Cups (Cancer Moon). Leo is ruled by the Sun and Cancer the Moon. So these two archetypes are extra strong for me being in their rulers. I don't connect that much at all with The Queen of Pentacles, which you may think I should with a Taurus Ascendant. People often say I appear as an earth mother (remember ascendants are how we appear, not necessarily how we are).

I hate cooking, housework, sewing or getting dirty or growing anything. (I have my very own King Of Pentacles to do that!) I do like being at home, but that is a Queen of Cups trait as well, and I do like animals as long as they are clean so I would never keep anything other than a cat, just like The Queen of Wands (but I am allergic to them!). I feel I connect more with The Queen of Swords than The Queen of Pentacles (much as I hate to admit it!). This maybe because the only other earth sign I have is Virgo in Mercury. Another sign also in its ruler, so very strong. You may think, but Virgo is Earth. Yes, but it's the most analytical aspect of earth, being ruled by Mercury which is also Gemini's ruler, therefore bringing out more Sword energy.

Notes:

Chapter 15

Reading

Please remember that the key to any reading is the ability to story-tell. The more you can do that, the less the need for spreads. The more you story tell the more your readings will flow and the less stagnant the positions.

All the exercises in the previous chapters are designed to ignite this ability, so make sure you have brought the cards alive through the exercises and storytelling diaries before you move on to actual readings. This way you are not just getting to know the characters in the Tarot but how the dynamics work together.

A common mistake in readings is placing the cards face down and then turning them over one at a time. How can you see the story? How can you see the dynamics relating to each other? Whether you are intuitively free flowing or doing a spread, the key below should help you with the navigation:

1 Make sure all the cards are face up.
2 How many Major Arcana?
3 Any repetitive numbers?
4 What grouping of numbers? (showing point in the cycle)
5 What's the balance of elements? (Cups, Swords, Pentacles and Wands)
6 What other similarities can you see linking the cards together?
7 If you have an overwhelming amount of court or Major Arcana cards that are making it hard to read then take another card for each with the intention that the next card will show you how the energy is expressing itself.

This will show the threads of the story. If you are free flowing you may now be able to run with your yarn. If you are using a spread, you have a firm foundation to go deeper into the positions.

Spreads

So let's start with the basic three card spread. You shuffled (and passed your cards to the client if you are reading for someone else). You then either dealt three cards of the top or spread the cards out and picked three.

Let's say that the first card is The Wheel Of Fortune, the second The Empress and the third The Four of Wands.

This would show that a change is coming the end, landing in The Empress. Being The Empress and Four of Wands this could be desire for a change of home or new arrival. But if we changed the last card for The Magician we wouldn't be landing at all! The change would be growing, life would be bursting everywhere and it would be very hard to pin it down to something due to the lack of the Minor Arcana.

To pin it down we take another card. Sometimes the card will be another major. If there are a lot of major, it shows that there are a lot of spiritual workings/hands of fate going on. But we intend and ask to be shown a minor.

If we get more major, we keep going and keep reading until we get a minor. So say the next card we get is The Eight of Pentacles that would show us that it's a great time for any changes we implement to our practical world. That there is a lot of fertility and creativity around for things to really grow fast, strong and well.

The only other spread you really need is of course the trusty Celtic cross. The way to read the Celtic differs from reader to reader but I like to see it as a living breathing tree, a bit like the Tree of Life. I will explain more with the positions below:

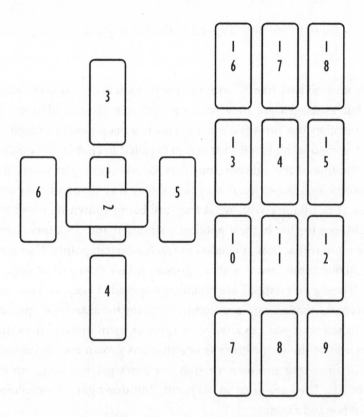

1 Is "I" the self in the present, the here and now. The present
   showing itself. The shrub bursting forth.
2 Is what crosses/aspects that current offering.
3 Is the height of the growth, the potential.
4 Is the foundation of the growth, the seed.
5 Is where the foundation came from, the tree the seed blew
   from, the past.
6 Is the future cycle of growth
   7, 8 and 9) Is a deeper look at the self (entering three card
   free flowing storytelling)
   10, 11 and 12) Is a deeper look at the environment
   13, 14 and 15) The subconscious, what messages you are
   sending to the universe.
   16, 17 and 18) The result of that. (Compare position 3 with

these to see how aligned to the truth of purpose the result is).

If someone isn't happy with the result look at the subconscious. What messages are they sending out? Are they in alignment? Remember the Tarot is a mirror. This is a deep look at oneself. If someone doesn't like it then action is called to change it. Looking at the line of the subconscious may clearly show you where the unconscious issues lie. It may not. Either way if you or someone else is not happy with what they are being shown then ask for guidance for the highest good of a situation and do a three card (or more if free flow is needed to reach a certain point). That way someone comes away with a signpost, rather than a dead end.

These two methods are mainly the spreads I keep to. They are my basic map. There are hundreds upon thousands of spreads out there and you can always create your own. Just like how this version of the Celtic cross is one that has grown and developed with time into my own version. So don't get too hung up on spreads. They are great to play with, but don't get overwhelmed and bogged down.

Awareness Guide
— When Reading for the Self, friends and family

Reading for the self is like a doctor doing self-diagnosis. It's a minefield. Nevertheless it's how a lot of us learn. So here are some tips to navigate the minefield:

When a doctor is ill, they can be the worst hypochondriac. They have too much knowledge. Ignorance is bliss! With no boundary, there is no comfort zone. The temptation to analyse over and over again can be all consuming. Eventually the doctor becomes confused, disempowered and un-centred. Fear has come in and we cannot tell truth from fear. A doctor protects the public from knowing too much, but does not have that protection himself. Because of the minefield of projections reading for yourself, friends or family is a lot harder than reading for strangers. But if you know how to navigate the mines, it can be an empowering experience. So make sure you have asked the following questions:

1) Why do you/they want a reading? Is it because you/they are upset or confused? (which is most likely). Just be aware that it may just mirror the confusion. Readings work best for everyone the calmer they are. Just like the clearest reflections are when the water is still.

2) Are you, your friend or family ready to take on board what comes up? If you are reading for a friend or family member, how will that alter your relationship? The Tarot is a mirror of your sub-conscious. It brings things up to the surface. There may be an awareness of it deep down, but are you or are they ready to face it? Are you ready to be that messenger in such an intimate relationship? When reading for strangers there is natural protection from the intimate dynamic. I have read for family in the past and it has been challenging to cope with what comes up. I have seen family secrets. Remember ignorance is bliss. I also have experience of this challenge on the personal level. I have seen the death of my own child, and the breakup of my long-term relationship. Sometimes you can't tell if it's your fear or the truth. You are just too close. It is not something to be taken lightly. Of course, you can always ask the best way forward for the situation. But are we normally that calm and level headed when emotionally involved?

3) Have you or they got to the point where just knowing (whatever the outcome may be) is better than not knowing? If so, the Tarot could help find clarity. But it still won't be easy. It is

hard to perceive yourself from the outside, similar to a goldfish trying to see its own bowl! Where as someone on the outside can see it clearly.

4) As the Tarot is primarily a mirror of your sub-conscious it reflects back to you your present state of mind. The worst thing you can do is discard it. The best thing you can do, is take whatever's shown on board, then do a further reading asking for the best way forward. A three card spread is good for this.

When reading for yourself, friends or family be aware of all of the above. Because the Tarot is a mirror, reading for yourself can be an uncomfortable experience. You may not like what you see. You may want to distort the reflection or dress it up. You may want to keep throwing the mirror away hoping to find the one that shows you the reflection you want. Before you know it you have you find yourself in an obsessive, disempowering cycle. A mirror is a mirror. It reflects only the truth, it can't change unless we do.

If the Tarot isn't treated with respect you will be giving your power to the Tarot. Your centre will belong to the Tarot and instead of being empowered you will feel disempowered, confused and dependent. Don't forget:

That we must practice seeing everything as a necessary step on the journey for the highest good.

If it shows you a pattern you don't like you can always ask why it's there and the best way forward.

Reading for others

May seem like the most scary option. How can you sit there and tell a complete stranger about themselves and their life? You have absolutely nothing to go on! No knowledge! Brilliant! This means no projections. A completely clear screen.

Your best readings are likely to be for complete and utter strangers for that very reason. You don't know them from Adam!

You have only your intuition to rely on as your mind knows nothing. Because your mind knows nothing the dangerous world of projection is minimised. The rating goes like this:

Reading for the self: most difficult.

Reading for partner or other close tie: almost as challenging.

Reading for friend: third hardest.

Reading for stranger: easiest.

Reading for return client: becoming harder.

Reading for regular: becoming harder still.

The Three Golden Rules

I opened my first practice next door to a rehab and alongside one of London's largest psychiatric hospitals. I had my work cut out! Knowing how dark times can draw people to the Tarot and being aware of the challenges there, I invented "The Three Golden Rules":

Positivity Not Negativity
Everything in life benefits you in some way, your task is to find that silver lining. Step back and see the beautiful tapestry being woven with the dark and light threads. Understand this. Eradicate the words "good" and "bad" from your vocabulary. Before I was a reader, I worked with children on the autistic spectrum with severely challenging behaviour. We were not allowed to use a negative phrase. "Stop doing that" was turned into "Put your hands on the table", "stop" or "no" did not give a direction, creating anxiety. The same principle applies here.

Healing Not Prediction.

Tarot is so tied up with prediction. People think Tarot and they think fortune-telling prediction. This is one side of the multi-faceted dice. The Tarot is so much more as hopefully this book has revealed to you. Remember it mirrors back your pattern. That is the only way it predicts. So are you going to use that to predict? If you do you run the risk of creating fear, or if it's a good prediction your run the risk of creating attachment. Or will you use the mirror to help people see? To help foster understanding of why they are in the cycle they are in? Once they have that, they may choose to take responsibility for the healing of their lives. That is the gift of true free will.

Of course, there is always the facet of prediction. But Prediction is not necessarily what you see but how you say it. For example if you see a break up, instead of saying, "I see a relationship ending" (prediction). You may say, "It looks like a rocky period coming up in your relationship, would you like to know the best way forward?" (Empowering/healing).

Empowerment Not Dependency

People generally come to readers when overwhelmed. Consequently, they may want you to take responsibility of their life. You will be asked, "should I do this?" "what do you think?". All you can do is tell them it is a mirror of what they think and what they feel and that you can help them see how they think and how they feel and explore the energy in possible situations. This can help them know how they are feeling about different options. Also keep your own empowerment, own statements with "I" "I see/ I feel" etc. They may disagree with you. But they cannot argue if you are stating that is the way you see it. They can only argue if you say they are like this, or their life is like that. These two tactics keep both of you empowered. This is important because you cannot empower another by disempowering yourself. We then have dependency minimised and also blame.

Now we finish on a lighter note!

Reading Tarot is a spiritual honour —

You get to see the most intimate depth of a soul.

Reading Tarot is magical —

What else shows you the patterns of life in a synchronistic way?

Reading the Tarot is exciting and fun —

As much as anxiety can exist with readings so does excitement — they are two sides of the same energy.

Reading the Tarot helps us develop intuition and strength —

To face the truth, for yourself and others and not bend in the face of it.

Reading the Tarot can help to transform lives for the better —

Not by telling people what they want to hear! But helping them to see the truth, only then can we transform.

Reading the Tarot is a spiritual practice of the silver lining —

Not the cloud.

Final Word

A life lived alongside the Tarot is one filled with depth, magic and meaning. Everything fits together and flows. Even when things are hard we are reminded that there is a higher purpose at work and that this too shall come to pass. When we see The Tower strike we can see it is the gift of enlightenment and we know we are on our way to The Star. We may even be able to see the higher purpose and understand it. Wherever understanding exists, confusion ends. Whenever confusion ends, pain ceases.

Eventually you will never need to give yourself a reading. Your intuition will be that honed. You will be able to read life. Remember the Tarot is the book of life. If you practice the exercises in this book, you will get to the point where you will meet someone and instantly know whether they are a King of Swords or Queen of Cups. You will see your dynamic and the message behind it. If you practice the exercises in this book enough you will see the situations in your life, therefore you will never need a reading. You will know how one cycle naturally flows into another...

In this way, Tarot becomes truly transformational.

Readings with or Learning with Tiffany

You can book Tiffany for a face to face or phone reading at Mysteries in Covent Garden on 0207 2403688. To see Tiffany face-to-face in Cornwall, or through Skype or phone, visit here: http://transcendentaltemple.co.uk/phone-readings.html

For details on Tiffany's courses and classes visit http://initiation workshops.co.uk/ where you can sign up to the newsletter to receive Tiffany's monthly AstroTarotChannel, a monthly blog of the Astrology for the coming month along with a YouTube video of the Tarot for the month, explained step by step.

Dodona Books offers a broad spectrum of divination systems to suit all, including Astrology, Tarot, Runes, Ogham, Palmistry, Dream Interpretation, Scrying, Dowsing, I Ching, Numerology, Angels and Faeries, Tasseomancy and Introspection.